Common
Occupational
Readiness
Essentials

CERTIFICATION PREP
Adobe InDesign Creative Cloud

by

D. Michael Ploor, MBA
National Board Certified Teacher
STEM Curriculum Integration Specialist
School District of Hillsborough County
Tampa, Florida

D1073584

Publisher
The Goodheart-Willcox Company, Inc.
Tinley Park, Illinois
www.g-w.com

Cover image: Lichtmeister/Shutterstock.com

Table of Contents

Introduction

The Common Occupational Readiness Essentials (CORE) series of certification preparation guides focuses on mastering the essential basic skills needed as a workplace-ready user of the software. The goal of each CORE certification preparation guide is to provide practice in each essential basic skill required by employers who use the software. To prove workplace readiness, you will also be prepared to take the official certification exam for the software.

CORE Adobe InDesign Creative Cloud will help prepare you to take the Adobe Certified Associate (ACA) Adobe InDesign Creative Cloud certification exam. It provides step-by-step instruction for the features and commands covered on the certification exam. The focus of the lessons is to practice *using* the actual commands and features instead of creating a complete end product. Most lesson content is created using the software, and minimal downloading of files is required. Furthermore, each certification preparation guide is broken down into small learning units to enable better comprehension and application of the software. Where required, answers are provided at the back of the certification preparation guide.

Certification as an Adobe Certified Associate demonstrates an aptitude with Adobe software. ACA certification is offered for Adobe Dreamweaver, Adobe Animate, Adobe Photoshop, Adobe Premier, Adobe Illustrator, and Adobe InDesign. Certification exams are provided by Certiport, Inc., through various testing facilities. Visit www.certiport.com for more information on registering for certification exams.

About the Author

D. Michael Ploor is the author of the CORE series of certification preparation guides. Mr. Ploor's students have achieved exceptional results with the CORE certification preparation guides. His students collectively pass more than 500 industry certification exams each year without the need for other preparation materials. Mr. Ploor has demonstrated the strength of integrating the CORE guides in a diverse mix of courses.

Mr. Ploor is also the author of three textbooks on the subject of video game design: *Introduction to Video Game Design, Video Game Design Foundations,* and *Video Game Design Composition.* He is a National Board Certified Teacher in Career and Technical Education and holds an MBA degree from the University of South Florida. He maintains professional teaching credentials in Business Education and Education Media Specialist.

Mr. Ploor is at the forefront of innovative teaching and curriculum. He developed STEM curriculum while serving as the lead teacher in the Career Academy of Computer Game Design at Middleton Magnet STEM High School. Mr. Ploor has applied his skills as a STEM Curriculum Integration Specialist in designing innovative curriculum and by collaborating to construct the state standards for video game design in several states. He has also been instrumental in authoring competitive events for Career and Technical Student Organizations such as the Future Business Leaders of America (FBLA) and Phi Beta Lambda (PBL).

In addition to publishing textbooks and lessons, Mr. Ploor provides professional development as a frequent presenter at regional and national conferences to promote CTE education and video game design curriculum.

Lesson 1
Typography and Layout

Objectives

Students will explain foundry type. Students will define typesetting terminology. Students will compare typeface and font. Students will illustrate type size and styling. Students will discuss readability.

Reading Materials

Adobe InDesign is a program specifically made for page composition. Page composition, or *layout*, is the placement of text, images, and objects in a document. Long before computer programs such as InDesign were available, text was created by placing individual blocks of movable type together to form each word. Blocks of text were further arranged into a layout to create paragraphs and columns. Images and other items were included in their final position before the entire layout was printed.

This form of movable type is called *foundry type*. Each letter is a block called a *sort*. The sorts are stored in a case, as shown in **Figure 1-1**. This job case, or type case, contains thousands of individual sorts for each letter or symbol needed. The letters in a job case are all of the same design, style, and size. Foundry type is composed by removing the individual letters from the case and placing them in a composing stick. The sorts are then moved from the composing stick into a *galley*. Eventually, there are enough words to fill a page and the galley is placed into a metal frame called a *chase*. From the chase, the type is placed in a *form*.

Setting foundry type is a lot of work and is very time-consuming. Thankfully, digital typesetting is now possible with powerful word processing programs such as Microsoft Word. This software allows a user to create multiple lines of text very quickly.

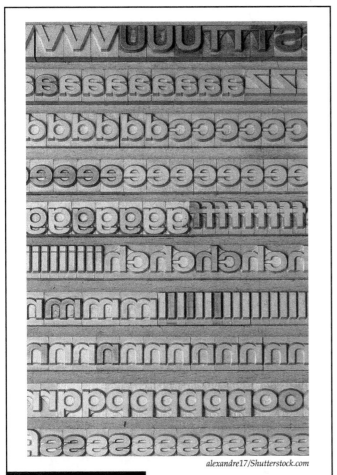

alexandre17/Shutterstock.com

Figure 1-1.

Individual letter blocks arranged in a typesetting case. Notice how the letters appear backward. This is so they appear right reading when pressed onto paper.

Typesetting Terminology

Some early typesetting terms have been carried into the digital age even though the technology they are based on is obsolete. Some of these terms include kerning, tracking, and leading.

Kerning is adjusting the spacing between special pairs of characters, as shown in **Figure 1-2.** When each individual sort block of foundry type is aligned in a chase row, it resembles the look of how kernels of corn are arranged in rows on a corn cob. So you can think of those tiny sort blocks as kernels. In some cases, unique sorts are created to make a more visually appealing pair of letters. Take the letters A and V. If placed as individual sorts next to each other, there appears to be too much space between them. Overlapping the A and V looks better. A special sort called a kern, or pair of letters sort block, solves this problem.

Tracking is the amount of space between all letters in a row of text, as shown in **Figure 1-2.** If you think about a set of railroad tracks, the timbers under the tracks are evenly spaced like the sorts in typesetting might be. If the timbers are spread out, the space between each timber along the track increases. This is like increasing the tracking on a line of type.

Leading is the amount of vertical space between lines of text. In foundry type, thin metal bars of lead are placed between the rows of type to control vertical spacing. Leading simply means adding lead. Depending on the thickness of the lead bar, single spacing, double spacing, or other custom spacing can be created between the rows of type and between paragraphs. Note, however, that in digital typesetting, leading is the distance from the baseline of one row of letters to the baseline of the next row of letters. In other words, it includes the height of letters, not just the space between lines of type.

VARIABLE
Unaltered

VARIABLE
Kerning Adjusted

VARIABLE
Tracking Adjusted

Goodheart-Willcox Publisher

Figure 1-2.

Kerning is the spacing between pairs of letters. Notice the positions of the V and the A. Tracking is the spacing between all characters.

Typeface

A *typeface* is a collection of letters, numbers, and symbols that are all of the same design. For example, Times New Roman and Helvetica are typefaces. A *font* is the set of characters within a typeface that are of one specific style and size. For example, Helvetica, bold, 10 point is a font. The typeface can be important in conveying meaning in a design project. Text set in one typeface may communicate elegance, while the same text set in a different typeface may communicate excitement or tension.

The two basic designs of typeface are serif and sans serif. *Serifs* are decorative marks at the end of letters, as shown in **Figure 1-3.** The word *sans* means without, so sans serif means without serif. There is much debate over which is more readable. Traditionally, serif type is used for long passages where readability is important, such as books, while sans serif type is used when legibility is important, such as street signs. However, there is no clear agreement among experts as to the significance between serif and sans serif type when it comes to readability and legibility. It is generally thought that a sans serif typeface promotes the feeling of security, trust, and strength, which is why this type is typically used in logos and headlines.

Other typefaces that fall outside of the serif or sans serif classification include novelty, ornate, handwritten, script, and ornamental. These are used as decoration or as an attention item on a page and should not be used when creating the body

TIP
Most computer software refers to the typeface as the font. Be aware this is not correct, and strive to use the proper terminology in conversations with peers and professionals.

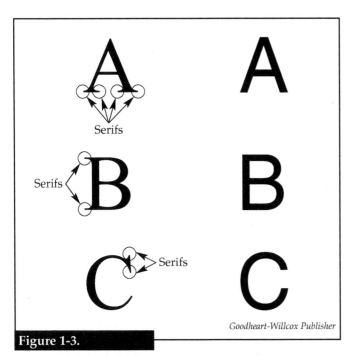

Goodheart-Willcox Publisher

Figure 1-3.

A comparison of serif and sans serif typefaces.

text. In addition to being hard to read, they may have the added problem of not being installed on the user's computer, which is important in web page design. If a digital device does not have a specified typeface installed, whether decorative, serif, or sans serif, it will display a substitute font.

Digital Type Size and Styling

Unlike foundry type that must fit in a rigid chase, digital type can be easily stylized and resized. In typesetting terminology, doing this is selecting the font of the typeface.

Changing the type size will create larger or smaller type. Type size is typically measured in points. *Point* is a unit of measure used in the publishing and graphic arts industries. There are 72 points in one inch. So, 9 point type is 1/8″ high. *Pica* is another unit of measure used in publishing and graphic arts. There are 12 points in one pica. Points and picas are often combined in a single measurement. For example, 2p5 means two picas and five points, which is a total of 29 points. In this notation, the pica value is always listed first. Leading is also measured in points, as are many other things, such as the size of images or the width of lines.

In addition to changing size, the style of a typeface can be changed. The most common typeface styles are **Bold,** *Italic,* and <u>Underline.</u> Stylizing does not change the basic design of the typeface, only alters the appearance of the type for emphasis. Notice how bold, italic type is used in this certification guide to emphasize key terms (vocabulary).

Other stylizing includes superscript and subscript. The fonts move the type vertically relative to the baseline. The *baseline* is an invisible line on which the type is placed. *Superscript* type is raised above the baseline, such as the 2 in X^2. *Subscript* type is lowered below the baseline, such as the 2 in H_2O. Superscript or subscript type is usually set in a smaller size as well as being adjusted from the baseline.

Digitally typeset text that has various size and styling applied is known as *rich text* and can be saved in a Rich Text Format (RTF) file. Digital text without any formatting is called plain text and can be saved as a TXT file.

Readability and Typeface Conflict

In the end, the function of a typeface is to allow the reader to actually read the text. The blocks of text need to be arranged into proper paragraphs, columns, and structures to provide readability. *Readability* is a measure of how easy or hard it is for a person to read the text. Proper punctuation and grammatical elements are also important components to readability.

When typefaces mix in a single document, the designer must avoid issues with typeface conflict. *Typeface conflict* occurs when two or more typefaces that are too similar are used in the same document. Examine the paragraph below. Can you find the typeface conflict?

This paragraph was written using the serif style typeface of Times New Roman. There are many serif style typefaces that look very similar. In this case, the typeface Century Schoolbook has been used for a portion of the paragraph. Notice how the subtle differences between the typefaces makes it look very odd and causes typeface conflict between the third sentence in this paragraph and all of the other sentences. Another conflict can occur as the final sentence was set in yet another typeface (Garamond).

Lesson 1 Review

Vocabulary

In a word processing document or on a sheet of paper, list all of the **key terms** in this lesson. Place each term on a separate line. Then, write a definition for each term using your own words. You will continue to build this terminology dictionary throughout this certification guide.

Review Questions

Answer the following questions. These questions are aligned to questions in the certification exam. Answering these questions will help prepare you to take the exam.

1. The purpose of InDesign is _____, which is another term for page composition.

   _____

2. What is the term for movable type consisting of sorts assembled into galleys, chases, and forms?

   _____

3. Which property of type adjusts the horizontal spacing between certain pairs of characters?

   _____

4. Which property of type evenly adjusts the horizontal spacing for *all* characters in a section of text?

   _____

5. What is the term for the vertical spacing between lines of text?

   _____

6. Describe the difference between a typeface and a font.

   _____

   _____

   _____

7. Which of the two basic typefaces does *not* contain decorative ends on the letters?

_____

8. Which type of font is used to promote a feeling of security and is typically used in headlines?

_____

9. What will occur if the user views a document containing a typeface that is not an installed font on the digital device he or she is using?

_____

_____

10. How many points are in one inch?

_____

11. What is the baseline for type?

_____

_____

12. Which file format can be used to save digital text without any formatting applied?

_____

13. Which file format can be used to save digital text with text styling applied?

_____

14. What does readability describe?

_____

_____

15. Describe typeface conflict.

_____

_____

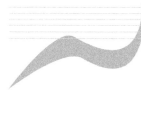

Lesson 2
Exploring the InDesign Interface

Objectives

Students will identify the trim, bleed, and margins in an InDesign document. Students will fill a text frame with placeholder text. Students will describe a workspace in InDesign. Students will recognize various tools in InDesign. Students will explain how layers are used in an InDesign document. Students will use the panel menu to complete various tasks. Students will discuss the use of smart guides. Students will explain how master pages are utilized in InDesign. Students will manage pages in a document. Students will apply paragraph and character formatting. Students will identify rulers and grids in InDesign. Students will create a custom workspace.

Situation

You have interviewed for a job as a layout artist and have been given a chance to participate in the apprentice program. To be hired as a full-time artist with the company, you will have to pass the Adobe Certified Associate (ACA) InDesign Creative Cloud industry certification exam. The first step in preparing for the exam is to gain experience using the functions of the software.

How to Begin

TIP
Adobe Creative Cloud provides running updates of the software. As a result, the version of the software you are using may be slightly different from the screen captures and tools illustrated in this certification guide.

TIP
The [Ctrl][N] key combination displays the **New Document** dialog box.

1. Before beginning this lesson, download the needed files from the student companion website located at www.g-wlearning.com, and unzip them into your working folder.

2. Launch Adobe InDesign Creative Cloud.

3. If a splash page or quick launch window appears, click the close button (**X**) in the top-right corner of the window to close it.

4. Locate the **File** pull-down menu on the menu bar at the top of the screen, and click **New…** in the menu (**File>New…**). A cascading menu appears showing the three types of designs that InDesign can create.
   - Document: a basic format for single-page and small multipaged documents
   - Book: a format used for large multipaged documents with chapters and a table of contents
   - Library: a storage container holding objects, images, templates, or snippets

5. Click **Document…** in the cascading menu. The **New Document** dialog box is displayed, as shown in **Figure 2-1.** The settings for the new document are listed along the right-hand side of the dialog box.

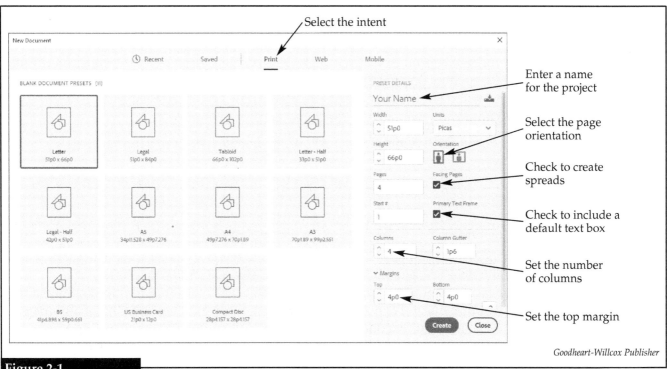

Figure 2-1.

Goodheart-Willcox Publisher

The **New Document** dialog box is used to set up and start a new InDesign document.

6. Click **Web** along the top of the dialog box. This is called the *intent.* The default values are filled in with what are typical for projects that will be output to a website. Notice the units of measurement are pixels.

7. Click **Print** along the top of the dialog box. This fills in default values that are typical for projects that will be printed on a printing press. Notice the units of measurement are picas.

8. Locate the **Margins** area along the right-hand side of the dialog box. Click the heading if needed to expand the area.

9. Replace the value in the **Top** text box with p48, and click in any other text box to set the value. The value of p48 is 48 points; the 0 in front of the p for pica is assumed. Notice that InDesign automatically converts the point value to 4 picas.

10. Click in the **Number of Pages** text box, and change the value to 4.

11. Make sure the **Facing Pages** check box is checked. When checked, the document will have pages in a spread. A *spread* consists of a left-hand page and the next right-hand page, like the facing left- and right-hand pages when you open a printed book or magazine.

12. Check the **Primary Text Frame** check box to add a text frame inside the document at the start.

13. Locate the **Start #** text box, and make sure the value is 1. This means the first page in the document will be numbered 1. Should you want to start at a different page number, simply enter it in this text box.

14. The default preset for page size in the **Print** intent is letter. This is the standard 8 1/2 inch by 11 inch sheet of paper you find in the desktop printer at your home or school. The page size can be changed by clicking a different preset on the left side of the dialog box or by manually entering values in the **Width** and **Height** text boxes on the right side of the dialog box. For this activity, select the letter size.

15. Locate the **Orientation** area on the right-hand side of the dialog box, and click the **Landscape** button. Notice the values for width and height have flip-flopped. *Landscape* orientation has the short edge of the page on the side like a flat screen television. *Portrait* orientation has the short edge of the paper on the top like a school portrait.

16. Click in the **Columns** text box, and change the value to 4. This is how many columns will be set up in the document.

17. Click in the **Column Gutter** text box, and enter 1p6. The *gutter* is the space between the columns.

18. Scroll down on the right-hand side of the dialog box, and click the **Bleed and Slug** heading to expand that area. *Bleed* is the area of the paper that is past the trim marks. A *slug* is an area in which to write specifications or other notes to the printer. It is also trimmed off the final paper.

19. Click in the **Top** text box under **Bleed**, and enter .5 in for 1/2 inch. Click in any other text box, and notice InDesign automatically converts the inch measurement into picas. Also, notice that all of the values for bleed changed at the same time. This is because the values are linked, as noted by the unbroken chain button to the right of the settings.

20. Click the unbroken chain button to the right of the bleed settings. The button changes to a broken chain to indicate the values are no longer linked.

21. Click in the **Outside** text box under **Bleed**, and enter 1.2 in.

22. Click the **Create** button to begin the document. A blank page is displayed containing empty text boxes arranged in four columns, as shown in **Figure 2-2**.

23. Click **File>Save** on the menu bar. Since the file has not yet been saved, the **Save As** dialog box is displayed. This is a standard save-type dialog box.

24. Navigate to your working folder.

25. The file name defaults to what was entered as the name of the project, but this can be changed. Click in the **File name:** text box, and enter *LastName_*Workspace.

26. Click the **Save as type:** drop-down arrow, and notice the various file types available. Click **InDesign Document (*.indd)** in the list, and then click the **Save** button. This will create an Adobe InDesign file that can be opened and manipulated in InDesign only.

Document

When a document is opened, you will see the InDesign workspace and the page on which to place your design. The document is the white page you see in the center of the screen.

27. Locate the black rectangle that outlines the document page. The black rectangle shows the trim. The *trim* is where the edge of the paper will be when it is cut to size after printing.

28. Locate the red rectangle outside the trim. The red rectangle shows the bleed area. The size of this rectangle is based on the bleed values you set when starting the document. Notice that the right side has a larger bleed area than all of the others. This is the slug area.

TIP

The [Ctrl][S] key combination can be used to quickly save a file. If the file has not yet been saved, the **Save As** function is launched.

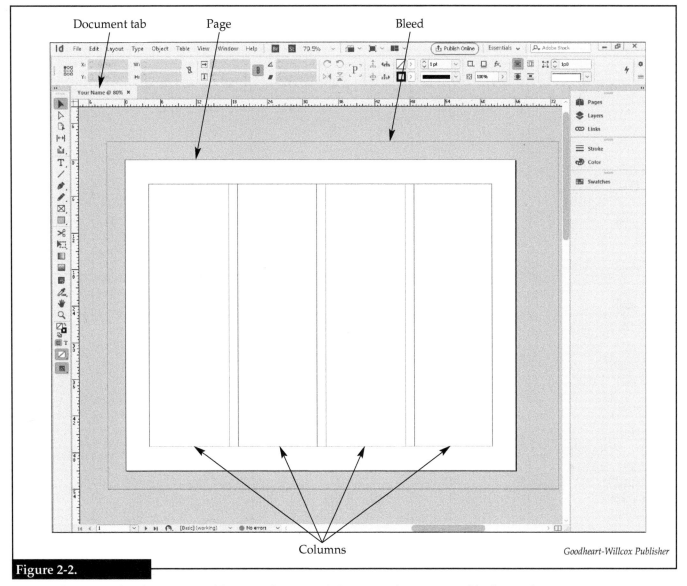

Document tab   Page   Bleed

Columns

Goodheart-Willcox Publisher

Figure 2-2.

A new document has been created in InDesign containing a text box arranged in four columns.

29. Locate and click one of the magenta (pink) lines inside the trim. The magenta lines show the margins of the document, and by clicking one of the margins, you have selected the default text frame that was included in the document setup. Notice the small boxes located around the rectangle. These are the resizing handles for the text frame.

30. Click and hold the handle at the top-center of the text frame, and drag it down near the center of the page. Notice the margin does not move as the text frame is resized. Also notice the text frame is indicated by blue lines.

31. Click the yellow-filled handle. The yellow handle is used to change the corners for a frame. Notice that there are now four yellow diamond handles, one in each corner.

32. Click and hold the yellow diamond in the top-right corner of the text frame, and drag it toward the top-center of the frame, and release, as shown in **Figure 2-3**. Notice that all four corners are now curved. There is a maximum curvature that can be applied.

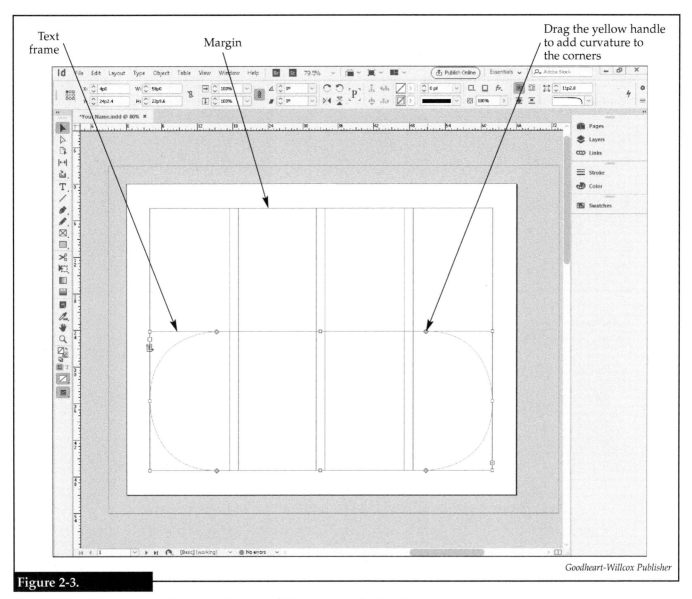

Text frame

Margin

Drag the yellow handle to add curvature to the corners

Goodheart-Willcox Publisher

Figure 2-3.

The yellow diamond handle is used to round the corners of a text frame.

Placeholder Text

Placeholder text is fake words and paragraphs used to fill text areas until the final text is provided. The purpose of placeholder text is to simply "hold the place" for the final text so you can continue to create a layout. Often, placeholder text is Greeked, which means it is not composed of real English words. This is also commonly referred to as *Lorem Ipsum* as those are the two "words" that usually appear at the beginning of the dummy text.

33. Click the text frame to select it.

34. Click **Type>Fill with Placeholder Text** on the **Application** bar (menu bar). The text frame is filled with Greeked text.

35. Use the scroll bar on the edge of the document area or the mouse wheel to scroll down to see the other pages in the document. Notice that all text frames are filled with placeholder text. The default text frames are all linked, so text will automatically flow from one text frame to the next.

Workspace

A *workspace* is the layout of the toolbars, panels, and document on the screen. Several standardized workspaces are available in InDesign, including workspaces such as Book and Digital Publishing. You may also create custom views by dragging the workspace tools to different locations and saving the workspace. Changing the layout by moving panels, adding more tools, rearranging panels, or otherwise changing the screen setup changes the workspace.

Review the location and name of each tool shown in **Figure 2-4.** These will be referred to by name throughout these lessons. Note: the color scheme shown in the screen captures in this guide has been changed to a lighter scheme for easy viewing.

The **Application** bar, or menu bar, holds the commands in a pull-down menu format. Click a pull-down menu to see the commands it contains, then click a command to activate it. This bar also contains the workspace switcher.

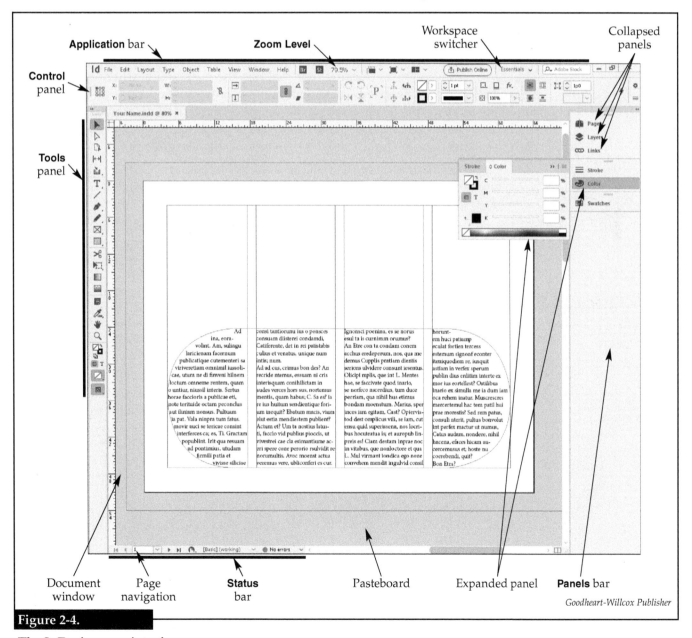

Goodheart-Willcox Publisher

Figure 2-4.

The InDesign user interface.

The **Control** panel contains some basic tools and a contextual toolbar. A contextual toolbar, panel, or menu contains options or features for the active tool or selected item. For example, if a line segment is selected, the **Control** panel displays settings for color, text wrapping, and transforms near the right-hand side of the panel.

The **Tools** panel holds the common tools used to design in InDesign. Tools are organized by function with a line separating each group.

InDesign makes use of panels. A panel is a small window that holds commands or options. A panel may be in a group by command function. A designer can arrange the panels in any configuration. The panels can even be moved from one panel group to another. Panels may be expanded with the commands visible or collapsed. Collapsed panels have been minimized to icons to save space on the screen. Clicking a panel icon will expand the panel.

The document tab displays the name of the document as well as the zoom percentage. The designer can have multiple documents open in InDesign at the same time. Each document will have a separate document tab. The designer can navigate between open documents by simply clicking the different document tabs. Dragging a document tab off the document tab area opens the document in a floating window.

The document window is the area that contains the page and is where text and images are placed. The area in the document window that is outside of the page is called the *pasteboard.* The pasteboard is not part of the final document. Anything on the pasteboard will not be printed. The pasteboard can be used as a holding place for items that need to be reused throughout the document.

36. Locate the **Zoom Level** setting on the **Application** bar, and click the drop-down arrow next to it. In the drop-down list, click **25%**. You should now be able to see all four pages on the three available spreads within the document window.

37. Locate the workspace switcher on the **Application** bar. It should be currently labeled Essentials. Click the workspace switcher, and notice the various workspaces available, as shown in **Figure 2-5**. Click Book in the drop-down list, and notice how the layout of the tools and panels has changed.

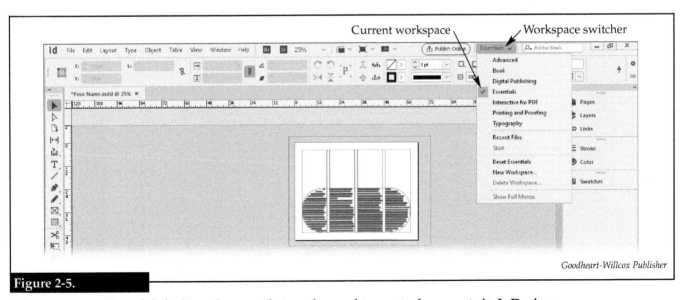

Goodheart-Willcox Publisher

Figure 2-5.
There are a number of default workspaces that can be used to create documents in InDesign.

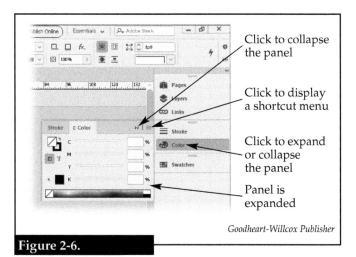

Click to collapse the panel

Click to display a shortcut menu

Click to expand or collapse the panel

Panel is expanded

Goodheart-Willcox Publisher

Figure 2-6.

The **Panels** bar contains collapsed panels that can be expanded. The **Panels** bar and the **Tools** panel are the two main means of accessing tools in InDesign.

38. Applying what you have learned, set the Essentials workspace current. Notice how the layout of the tools and panels has changed back to what it was.

39. Click the bar at the top of the **Tools** panel, hold, and drag the panel to the middle of the screen. This panel is now *floating,* whereas before it was *docked.*

40. Click the **Color** button in the **Panel** bar on the right side of the screen. The panel changes from *collapsed* to *expanded,* as shown in **Figure 2-6.** Notice that one other panel—**Stroke**—is nested in the expanded panel along with the **Color** panel. Clicking the name of either panel brings that panel to the front.

41. Click the double chevron button (**>>**) in the top-right corner of the **Color** panel. This collapses the panel.

42. Click the workspace switcher, and click **Reset Essentials** in the drop-down list. This returns the Essentials workspace to the default settings. The changes you make are automatically saved to the current workspace, and resetting the workspace basically undoes those changes.

Tools

The InDesign **Tools** panel contains buttons for various tools, which are organized in groups. Some tools have similar tools hidden under the tool shown by the button. A black triangle at the bottom-right corner of a button indicates that clicking the button will display a flyout. A *flyout* is a hidden toolbar that will "fly out" and be displayed like a panel. Clicking and holding a flyout button displays the flyout from which additional tools can be selected. A single click on the button will activate the tool displayed by the button without displaying the flyout.

43. Identify each of the tools shown in **Figure 2-7.** Hover the cursor over each tool in the **Tools** panel to display the name, and record the name of each tool in the figure. In some cases, you will need to click and hold the button to display the flyout in order to see the tool.

	Icon	Name		Icon	Name
1.			4.		
2.			5.		
3.			6.		

Goodheart-Willcox Publisher

Figure 2-7.

Write the name of each tool identified here.

	Icon	Name		Icon	Name
7.	T		22.	⬡	
8.	⤵		23.	✂	
9.	/		24.	◤	
10.	✒		25.	↻	
11.	＋✒		26.	⬀	
12.	✒		27.	⬈	
13.	Λ		28.	◼	
14.	✏		29.	▦	
15.	✎		30.	🗐	
16.	✐		31.	✎	
17.	⊠		32.	⟍	
18.	⊗		33.	✐	
19.	⬗		34.	✋	
20.	◻		35.	🔍	
21.	⬭				

Figure 2-7.

Continued.

44. Identify each of the tools shown in **Figure 2-8.** Record the name of each tool in the figure. The name of each tool appears next to the icon in the **Panels** bar.

45. Applying what you have learned, change the zoom level to 100%. Use the scroll bars along the side and bottom of the document window to center the first page on the screen. You may need to use a different zoom level for the entire page to fit in the document window.

	Icon	Name		Icon	Name
1.	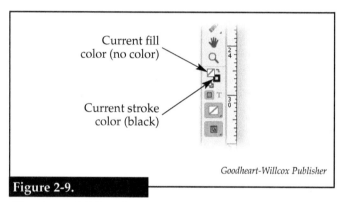		5.		
2.			6.		
3.			7.		
4.					

Figure 2-8.

Goodheart-Willcox Publisher

Write the name of each tool identified here.

Rectangle

46. Click the **Rectangle Tool** button in the **Tools** panel. The tool is activated, and the cursor changes to a crosshair or plus sign.

47. Click anywhere on the page near the top-left corner above the text frame, hold down the mouse button, and drag a rectangle about one-quarter the size of the page. When the mouse button is released, the rectangle is created and automatically filled with the current fill color and outlined with the current stroke color. The current fill and stroke colors appear in swatches at the bottom of the **Tools** panel, as shown in **Figure 2-9.** If the current fill color is white, the rectangle may not appear to be filled because the page is white, but it is filled. However, if there is no current fill color set, as indicated by a slash through the color swatch, the rectangle is not filled, and anything behind it will be visible. Also notice the **Control** panel has changed to display options for the selected shape (the rectangle).

Current fill color (no color)

Current stroke color (black)

Goodheart-Willcox Publisher

Figure 2-9.

The current fill and stroke swatches indicate the color that will be used for new shapes.

48. Double-click the color swatch in the **Tools** panel for the fill color. The **Color Picker** dialog box is displayed, as shown in **Figure 2-10.**

49. Using the **C:**, **M:**, **Y:**, and **K:** text boxes, enter values for 100% cyan, 50% magenta, 10% yellow, and 30% key (black). This creates a dark blue, as reflected in the preview. Click the **OK** button to change the fill color swatch and to apply the color as a fill for the rectangle.

50. Applying what you have learned, change the stroke color to C0, M0, Y100, K0. The stroke may be very thin, so you may need to zoom in on the rectangle to see the color change.

Selection Tool

51. Click the **Selection Tool** button in the **Tools** panel. Then, click the rectangle to make sure it is selected. When selected, the rectangle will have handles displayed, just like when the text box was selected earlier.

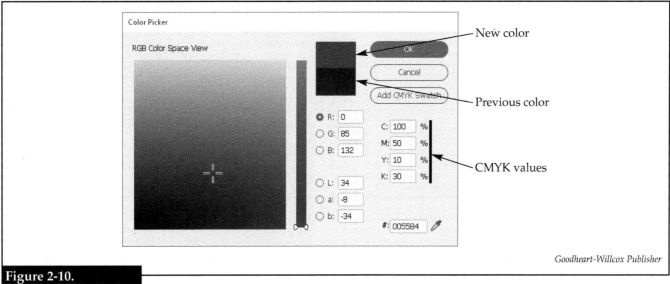

Goodheart-Willcox Publisher

Figure 2-10.

Creating a new color using the **Color Picker** dialog box.

The swatches available in the drop-down menu in the **Control** panel are also available in the **Swatches** panel.

New Swatch

52. In the **Control** panel, click the arrow next to the fill color swatch. The fill color swatch is dark blue, just like it is in the **Tools** panel. When the arrow is clicked, a drop-down menu is displayed containing several color swatches, as shown in **Figure 2-11.** Make note of the available swatches.

53. In the tools at the bottom of the drop-down menu, click the **New Swatch** button. This adds the current fill color (dark blue) as a new swatch in the menu. Press the [Esc] key to close the drop-down menu.

54. Click the arrow next to the stroke color swatch on the **Control** panel, and click the black color swatch. This changes the stroke color on the selected object and sets the current stroke color. A stroke is a line shape or the outline of a shape.

55. Click the collapsed **Stroke** panel in the **Panel** bar to expand it. Notice that some of the commands in this panel are also available on the **Control** panel.

56. Click in the **Weight:** text box in the **Stroke** panel, and enter 6 pt. This sets the weight to six points. *Weight* is the thickness of the stroke. Notice the outline of the rectangle is now much thicker.

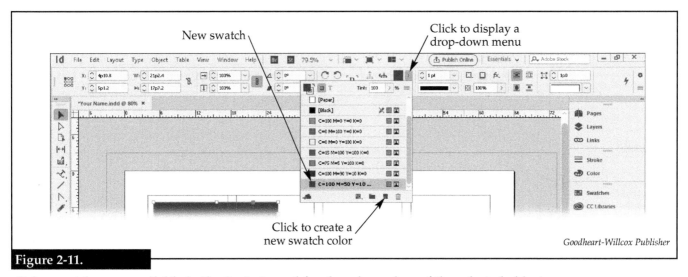

Goodheart-Willcox Publisher

Figure 2-11.

Color swatches are available in the **Control** panel for changing colors of the selected object.

57. Click the **Type:** drop-down arrow on the **Stroke** panel, and click **Dashed (3 and 2)** in the drop-down list. The stroke is changed from a solid line to a dashed line.

58. Click the **Gap Color:** drop-down arrow in the **Stroke** panel, and click **C=0 M=0 Y=100 K=0** in the drop-down list. This is pure yellow. The stroke should now be a black and yellow dashed line where the black section is one-third larger than the yellow.

59. Locate the **W:** and **H:** text boxes on the **Control** panel. The values in these text boxes set the width and height of the selected object. Enter 58p0 in the **W:** text box and 14p0 in the **H:** text box.

60. With the **Selection Tool** active, click and drag the rectangle so it touches the top, left, and right margin guidelines, as shown in **Figure 2-12.**

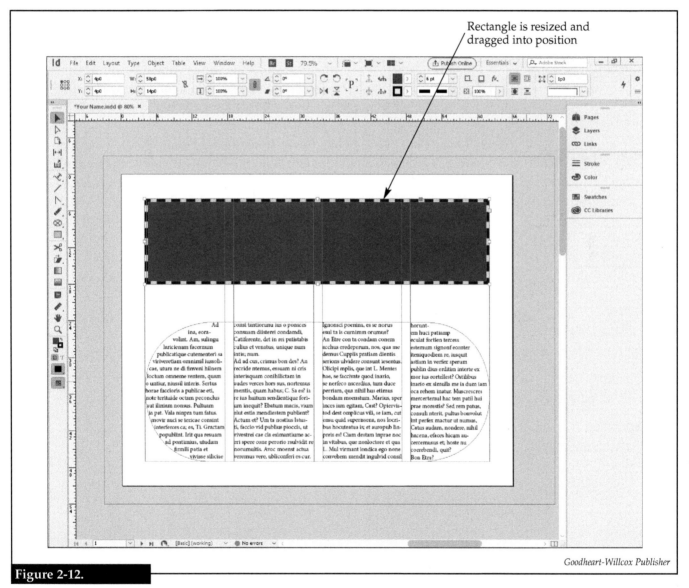

Rectangle is resized and dragged into position

Goodheart-Willcox Publisher

Figure 2-12.

Use the **Selection Tool** to move the rectangle into position.

Layers

Layers are like invisible sheets of paper stacked on top of each other, and each sheet can have different drawing shapes placed on it. The layers can be moved up or down within the layers stack to change the placement of shapes. Shapes placed on the top layers will appear in front of shapes on the bottom layers. The **Layers** panel is used to rearrange the order of layers in the stack. When working with drawing objects, the layers help arrange objects above or beneath each other. To make this work, each object must be drawn on a separate layer. The layers can then be moved within the layers stack so each is in the correct placement on top of or below other objects.

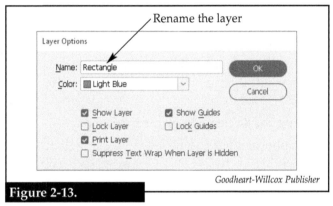

Rename the layer

Goodheart-Willcox Publisher

Figure 2-13.

A layer can be renamed in the **Layer Options** dialog box.

New

Ellipse Tool

Selection Tool

61. Click the **Layers** panel in the **Panels** bar to expand it.

62. The default layer is named Layer 1. Double-click on the name to open the **Layer Options** dialog box, as shown in **Figure 2-13.**

63. In the **Layer Options** dialog box, click in the **Name:** text box, and change the name to Rectangle. Then, click the **OK** button to rename the layer.

64. In the **Layers** panel, click the **New** button. A new layer is added to the list.

65. Single-click twice (two slow clicks) on the name of the new layer to make the name editable. Then, rename the layer as Circle. Press the [Enter] key to set the name.

66. Make sure the Circle layer is current. The current layer is highlighted in the **Layers** panel. A pen icon also indicates the current layer, as shown in **Figure 2-14.**

67. Click the **Ellipse Tool** button in the **Tools** panel. This is located in the flyout displayed by clicking and holding the **Rectangle Tool** button.

68. Hold down the [Shift] key, then click and drag to draw a circle of any size on page 1. Holding the [Shift] key while drawing an ellipse constrains the shape to a circle.

69. In the **Control** panel, click the chain icon next to the **W:** and **H:** settings to lock the values. This will keep the shape as a circle when either value is changed.

70. Applying what you have learned, change the width to 1.5 inches. The **W:** and **H:** settings should both automatically update to 9p0.

71. Applying what you have learned, fill the circle with the dark blue you created earlier.

72. Applying what you have learned, use the **Selection Tool** to drag the circle so it is near the center of the text frame on page 1. Notice how the fill color of the circle blocks the text behind the circle.

73. In the **Layers** panel, click and hold the Circle layer, and drag and drop it below the Rectangle layer in the list. Notice how the circle now appears beneath the text on the page. The text frame is located on the Rectangle layer, which is now above the Circle layer in the layer stack.

74. Applying what you have learned, select the rectangle.

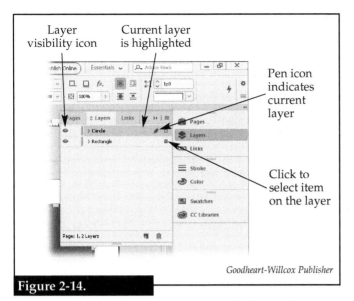

Layer visibility icon

Current layer is highlighted

Pen icon indicates current layer

Click to select item on the layer

Goodheart-Willcox Publisher

Figure 2-14.

The **Layers** panel is used to manage the layers in the document.

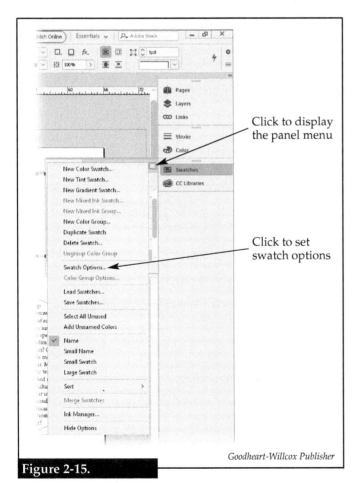

Click to display the panel menu

Click to set swatch options

Goodheart-Willcox Publisher

Figure 2-15.

Using a panel menu.

75. Click the **Swatches** panel in the **Panels** bar to expand it. Then, click the None swatch. This swatch is white with a red slash. Setting the fill color to None removes the fill.

76. Using the **Selection Tool**, try to select the circle. Notice how each time you try to click the circle, the text frame is selected. This is because the layer the text frame is on is above the layer containing the circle. The **Layers** panel needs to be used to manage the layers.

77. In the **Layers** panel, click the **Toggles visibility** button (eye) to the left of the Rectangle layer. Everything on that layer is hidden, which includes the rectangle and the text frame.

78. Applying what you have learned, select the circle and change the fill color to red (C15, M100, Y100, K0).

79. Drag the circle to the top-center of page 1.

80. Applying what you have learned, toggle the visibility of the Rectangle layer so it is visible. Notice how the circle is visible because the fill color has been removed from the rectangle.

81. In the **Layers** panel, click in the space between the **Toggles visibility** button and the name of the Rectangle layer. A lock icon appears. The Rectangle layer is now locked and cannot be edited.

82. Click the lock icon for the Rectangle layer to unlock the layer. The layer can once again be edited.

Panel Menu

Most panels have a panel menu. This menu contains additional commands not displayed as buttons or settings in the panel. The panel menu button is located in the top-right corner of the panel.

83. With the **Selection Tool** active, click any empty space in the document to deselect anything that is selected.

84. Click the **Swatches** panel in the **Panels** bar to expand it, scroll down, and select the dark blue color swatch you created earlier.

85. Click the panel menu button in the top-right corner of the panel to display the menu options, as shown in **Figure 2-15**. Notice there are options to add special swatches, such as tint swatches and gradient swatches.

86. Click **Swatch Options...** in the panel menu. The **Swatch Options** dialog box is displayed.

87. Uncheck the **Name with Color Value** check box. The **Swatch Name:** text box is enabled. A name can now be entered.

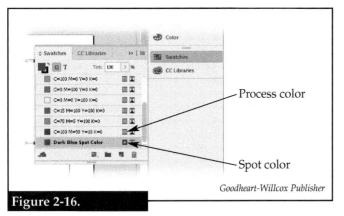

Process color

Spot color

Goodheart-Willcox Publisher

Figure 2-16.

Icons indicate if a color swatch is a spot color or a process color.

88. Enter Dark Blue Spot Color as the name.

89. Click the **Color Type:** drop-down arrow, and click **Spot** in the list. Remember, spot means this color will not be a CMYK blend. Rather, it will be printed using this exact color of ink.

90. Click the **OK** button to rename the color and update it as a spot color. Notice the icon to the right of the Dark Blue Spot Color swatch now has a spot in it to indicate that it is a spot color, as shown in **Figure 2-16.**

91. Applying what you have learned, display the panel menu for the **Swatches** panel, and click **New Gradient Swatch...** in the menu. The **New Gradient Swatch** dialog box is displayed, as shown in **Figure 2-17.**

92. Click in the **Swatch Name:** text box, and enter Yellow Fade.

93. Click the **Type:** drop-down arrow, and click **Radial** in the list. A *radial gradient* starts at the center and moves toward the edges in all directions in a circular fashion. A *linear gradient* follows a straight line.

94. Locate the gradient ramp at the bottom of the dialog box. This shows the color points for the gradient. Click the node, or color stop, on the left edge of the gradient ramp. The color settings in the dialog box are enabled. The settings are for the color at this node.

95. Change the color values to C0, M0, Y100, K0.

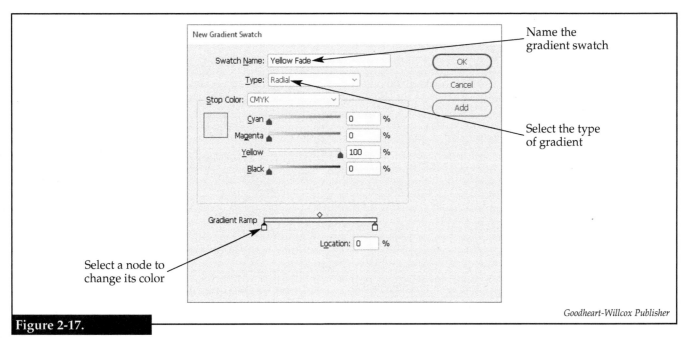

Name the gradient swatch

Select the type of gradient

Select a node to change its color

Goodheart-Willcox Publisher

Figure 2-17.

Creating a radial gradient fill.

96. Click the node on the right side of the gradient ramp. The **Stop Color:** drop-down list should automatically change to Swatches. If not, click the drop-down arrow, and click **Swatches** in the list.

97. Click the Paper color swatch. Notice how the yellow fades away on the gradient ramp. In practice, white is created in printing by leaving the paper area blank. There is not a color swatch for white in CMYK.

98. Click the **OK** button to create the gradient color swatch.

99. Applying what you have learned, remove the stroke color from the circle and change the fill color to the new gradient you just created.

Smart Guides

Smart guides are guidelines, locations, and comments that appear to help the designer properly align objects. They are temporary guides and can be turned on or off. They are on by default.

100. Click **View>Grids & Guides** on the **Application** bar. A cascading menu is displayed. Make sure the **Smart Guides** menu item is checked. When checked, smart guides are enabled.

101. Applying what you have learned, select the circle and drag it across the rectangle. Smart guides appear when alignment points on the circle match those of the rectangle or the page.

102. Using the smart guides, align the circle so its center is at the vertical and horizontal center of the rectangle, as shown in **Figure 2-18.** A green smart guide indicates the object is vertically centered, and a red smart guide indicates the object is horizontally centered.

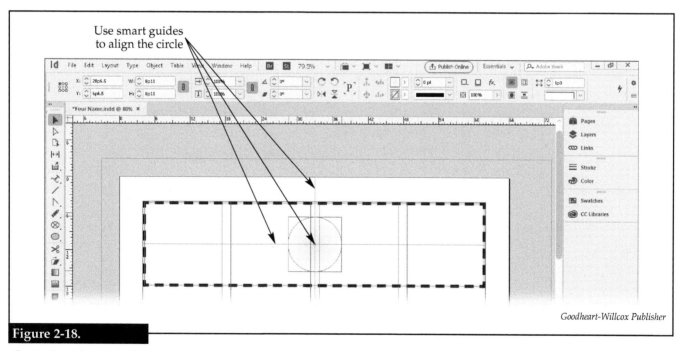

Goodheart-Willcox Publisher

Figure 2-18.

Centering the circle in the rectangle using smart guides.

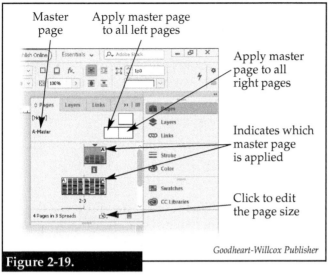

Master page | Apply master page to all left pages
Apply master page to all right pages
Indicates which master page is applied
Click to edit the page size

Goodheart-Willcox Publisher

Figure 2-19.

The **Pages** panel is used to manage document pages and master pages.

Pages Panel

Probably the most important panel in InDesign is the **Pages** panel. This panel allows the designer to set up master pages and arrange the document pages. A *master page* is a template that can be applied to document pages. The designer can create different custom layout profiles for each master page.

103. Applying what you have learned, change the zoom level to 50% so you can see more document pages on the screen.

104. Click the **Pages** panel in the **Panels** bar to expand it. Notice that the top section of the panel states A-Master and the bottom section shows the page spreads with an A at the top of each page, as shown in **Figure 2-19**. The first master page is A-Master, the next is B-Master, and so on.

105. In the top section of the **Pages** panel, click the right-side page of the A-Master spread. This selects the right-hand page of the A-Master page.

Edit Page Size

106. Click the **Edit Page Size** button at the bottom of the **Pages** panel, and click **Legal** in the drop-down menu. Notice that all of the right-hand pages in the document update to match the master page. The orientation also changes, as the default orientation for this setting is landscape.

107. Click **Edit>Undo Resize Item** on the **Application** bar. The edit to the master page is reversed, and the right-hand pages in the document return to letter size in landscape orientation.

Create New Page

108. With the right side of the A-Master page selected, click the **Create New Page** button at the bottom of the **Pages** panel. A new master page, B-Master, is created and added to the **Pages** panel. A new, empty page spread is also displayed in the document window.

109. Double-click on page 1 (or any page) in the spread section of the **Pages** panel to return to the working document.

110. Double-click the right side A-Master page in the **Pages** panel. Any changes made now will be applied to all right-hand pages in the document based on the A-Master page. You can tell you are editing the master page because the document text is hidden and only one spread is displayed.

Type Tool

111. Click the **Type Tool** button in the **Tools** panel. Then, click in the bottom-right corner of the right-hand page between the margin guide and the trim edge of the paper, and drag to create a text box.

112. Click the selection tool, and then, using the **Control** panel, change the width and height settings to 4p0 each. Make sure the settings are not locked, otherwise changing one setting affects the other.

113. On the **Application** bar, locate the **X:** and **Y:** text boxes. These text boxes contain the coordinate values for the location of the text frame on the page. Enter 128p0 in the **X:** text box and 47p0 in the **Y:** text box. This locates the text frame in the lower-right corner of the page.

 Copyright Goodheart-Willcox Co., Inc.

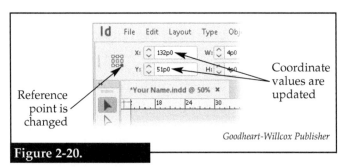

Coordinate values are updated

Reference point is changed

Goodheart-Willcox Publisher

Figure 2-20.

The reference point for an object can be changed to help with alignment.

Type Tool

Selection Tool

TIP
The [Ctrl][C] key combination can be used to copy an object. The [Ctrl][V] key combination can be used to paste an object.

114. Notice the grid to the left of the **X:** and **Y:** text boxes on the **Control** panel, as shown in **Figure 2-20.** This is the reference point matrix. The *reference point* is the location on a frame or object where the X and Y coordinates are located. By default, the reference point is in the top-left corner. Click the lower-right node in the matrix to move the reference point to that location. Notice how the X and Y coordinate values automatically adjust to reflect the location of the reference point.

115. Click the **Type Tool** button, and click inside the text frame. A flashing vertical cursor indicates text can be added to the frame.

116. Click **Type>Insert Special Character>Markers>Current Page Number** on the **Application** bar. This automatically adds a code that will display the correct page number when the document is viewed.

117. Double-click the page 3 thumbnail in the **Pages** panel. Notice how the correct page number is displayed where the text frame was added on the master page. Also, notice a page number appears on page 1. Any right-hand page based on the A-Master page will have a page number in this location. However, the left-hand pages do not have any page numbers because that has not been set up on the master page.

118. Applying what you have learned, display the A-Master page for editing.

119. Click the **Selection Tool** button, and click the text frame containing the page number code on the right-hand page.

120. Click **Edit>Copy** on the **Application** bar. This places a copy of the text frame on the system clipboard.

121. Click **Edit>Paste** on the **Application** bar. A copy of the original text frame is placed on the page.

122. Using the **Select Tool**, drag the new text frame to the lower-left corner on the left-hand page.

123. Applying what you have learned, display the document pages. Notice how page 2 now has a page number.

124. Using the **Select Tool**, try to select the text frame for the page number. You cannot select the frame because it is placed on the master page. Anything on the master page can only be selected or changed when editing the master page.

Managing Pages Using the Pages Panel

The order of pages in a document can be easily changed. The **Pages** panel is used to do this. Rearranging pages in InDesign is much like rearranging slides in PowerPoint.

125. Open the **Pages** panel.

126. Click the thumbnail for page 1, drag it to the position of page 3, and release the mouse button. Page 1 is dropped into page 3 position and pages 2 and 3 are moved up to be pages 1 and 2. Notice that the page numbers automatically update to reflect the new positions of the pages.

Enter the number for the first page in the section

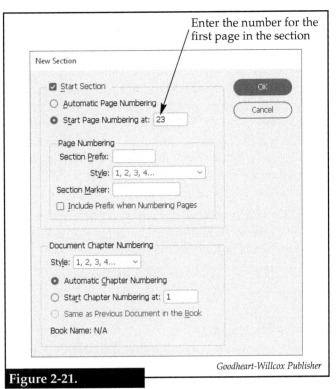

Figure 2-21.

Changing the page numbering for a new section in the document.

Edit Page Size

127. Double-click the thumbnail for new page 3 in the **Pages** panel to select only that page of the document. The thumbnail for the right-hand page of the spread should be highlighted in blue. This also navigates the view in the document window to the selected page.

128. Click the panel menu button in the top-right corner of the **Pages** panel, and click **Numbering & Section Options...** in the menu. The **New Section** dialog box is displayed, as shown in **Figure 2-21.** A new section is started in the document beginning with the page selected in the **Pages** panel. A section is simply a dividing point in the document. For example, the first few pages may have page numbers set as roman numerals, while the rest of the document has page numbers set as Arabic numerals.

129. Click the **Start Page Numbering at:** radio button, and enter 23 in the associated text box. Then, click the **OK** button to create the section. Notice the page numbers on the document spread are now page 2 on the left and page 23 on the right.

130. Select page 23 in the **Pages** panel, click the panel menu button, and click **Duplicate Page** in the menu. The new page is placed at the end of the document, which in this case is page 25.

131. Select the thumbnail for page 25 in the **Pages** panel. Then, click the menu panel button, and click **Delete Page** in the menu. A message appears warning that the selected page contains objects. Click the **OK** button to delete the page.

132. Select the thumbnail for page 23 in the **Pages** panel, and click the **Edit Page Size** button at the bottom of the panel, and click **Custom...** in the menu. The **Custom Page Size** dialog box is displayed.

133. Change the **Width:** to 35 centimeters or 35cm, and click the **OK** button to change the page size. InDesign automatically converts centimeters to picas and points.

134. Applying what you have learned, resize the text frame and the rectangle so they both touch the right margin on page 23. Also, move the gradient-filled circle so it is again in the center of the rectangle.

Paragraph and Character Formatting

Notice that the page number on page 2 is nearest to the edge of the paper and the page number for page 23 is away from the edge of the paper. The page numbers on the left-hand pages need to be adjusted. This is done with the **Paragraph** panel. The **Paragraph** panel is used to make alignment changes to entire paragraphs of text. The formatting of characters can be changed using the **Character** panel.

135. Applying what you have learned, select the left-hand A-Master page for editing, and select the text frame on that page.

TIP

The [Ctrl][Alt][T] key combination can be used to display the **Paragraph** panel.

136. Click **Type>Paragraph** on the **Application** bar. The **Paragraph** panel is displayed in a floating state.

137. Click and hold the top bar of the **Paragraph** panel, drag the panel to the **Panels** bar, and drop it just below the **CC Libraries** panel. A horizontal line appears on the **Panels** bar where the panel will be placed as you drag it. The panel is now docked and collapsed.

138. Click the **Paragraph** panel to expand it.

139. Click **Type>Character** in the **Application** bar. The **Character** panel is displayed in a floating state.

140. Applying what you have learned, dock the **Character** panel next to the expanded **Paragraph** panel, as shown in **Figure 2-22**. The expanded panel will be highlighted to indicate that the panel will be joined to form a new panel group with two tabs. Panels can be docked to any other panel group or floated as their own panel.

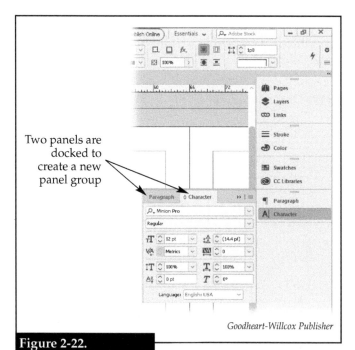

Two panels are docked to create a new panel group

Goodheart-Willcox Publisher

Figure 2-22.

Panels can be docked together to create a new group. Panels can also be moved within the **Panels** bar or floated.

Align right

TIP

Paragraph and character changes can also be performed using the **Control** panel in paragraph or character mode. You will have practice using those features in later lessons.

141. Click the tab for the **Paragraph** panel to bring that panel to the front.

142. Hover the cursor over the buttons at the top of the **Paragraph** panel to display the help text for each. Then, click the **Align right** button. Notice that the page number code in the text frame is aligned to the top right of the text frame.

143. Click the **Type Tool** button, and select the page number code in the text frame.

144. Applying what you have learned, display the **Character** panel.

145. Click the second drop-down arrow, which should currently say **Regular**, and click **Bold** in the drop-down list. This sets the style of the typeface.

146. Click in the **Font Size** text box, and enter 36 pt.

147. Copy the page number code in the frame on the left-hand page, and paste it into the text frame on the right-hand page, replacing the existing code. Change the alignment to left.

148. Display the document pages. Notice how the page numbers are now formatted.

Showing Rulers and Grids

InDesign has several helper objects. You have already seen how smart guides can be used to help align objects. Rulers and grids are also helper objects. They can be used to align objects on the page. Rulers are displayed by default, but the grids are not.

149. Click **View>Hide Rulers** on the **Application** bar. This will remove the rulers if not needed.

150. Click **View>Show Rulers**. Rulers are displayed along the top and left-hand side of the document window.

151. Move the cursor around the document window and look at the rulers. Notice how there are dotted or dashed lines on each ruler to tell you where the cursor is at any time.

152. Right-click anywhere on the top ruler, and click **Centimeters** in the shortcut menu. This shortcut menu can be used to change the units of measure for the ruler and to change how the ruler behaves.

153. Click **View>Grids & Guides** on the **Application** bar. Notice there are three different grids that can be displayed, as shown in **Figure 2-23**. Click **Show Document Grid** in the cascading menu. The grid is displayed in the document window. Grids help the designer align to the ruler and position graphics on the spread.

154. Click **View>Grids & Guides>Hide Document Grids**. The document grid is turned off.

Grids that can be displayed

Document grid is displayed

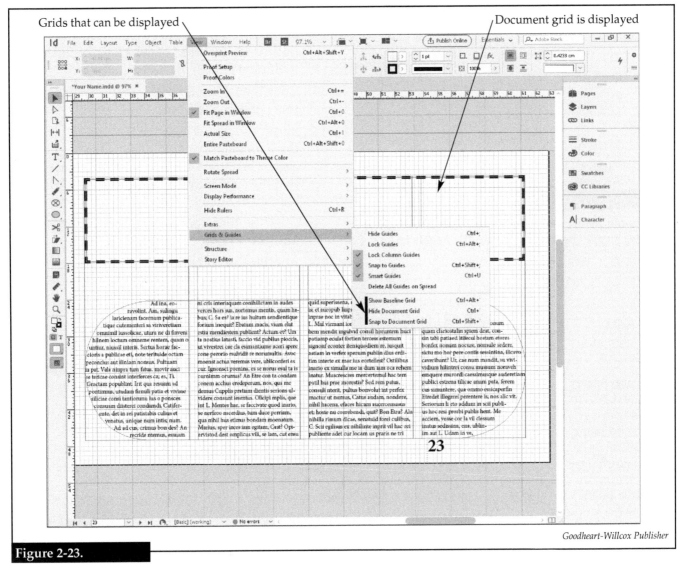

Goodheart-Willcox Publisher

Figure 2-23.

Grids are helper objects that can be displayed to help align objects.

Custom Workspace

To this point, you have used the default Essentials workspace layout. However, most users find they like to customize the workspace to have the tools and panels in locations that suit them best and how they work.

155. Click the **Paragraph** panel in the **Panels** bar, and drag it away from the collapsed panels. This floats the panel. If the panel was collapsed, it will be collapsed as a floating panel.

156. If the floating panel is collapsed, click the double chevron button (**>>**) next to the panel menu button to expand the panel.

157. Applying what you have learned, float the **Character** panel.

158. Click the close button (**X**) on the **Character** panel. The panel is hidden.

159. Click **Edit>Preferences>General…** on the **Application** bar. The **Preferences** dialog box is displayed.

160. Select **Units & Increments** on the left side of the dialog box. Then, on the right side, click the **Horizontal:** drop-down arrow, and click **Inches** in the drop-down list. This changes the units for the horizontal ruler to inches and all measurements to inches instead of picas.

161. Click **Spelling** on the left side of the dialog box, and check the **Enable Dynamic Spelling** check box. This setting will quickly allow you to see misspelled words in the document as they will be underlined in red. Other errors will be underlined in green.

TIP
The colors for errors can be changed in the **Preferences** dialog box.

162. Click the **OK** button to set the preference changes and close the dialog box. Notice how all of the words in the document are underlined in red. This is because the placeholder text does not contain recognized words. Therefore, InDesign thinks they are misspelled.

163. Click the workspace switcher button on the **Application** bar, and click **New Workspace…** in the drop-down menu. The **New Workspace** dialog box is displayed.

164. Click in the **Name:** text box, and enter Floating Paragraph Panel. Then, click the **OK** button to save the workspace. Notice that the new workspace is automatically set as the current workspace.

165. Applying what you have learned, set the Essentials workspace current, and reset the workspace. Notice the **Paragraph** panel is no longer displayed.

166. Applying what you have learned, set the Floating Paragraph Panel workspace current. The **Paragraph** panel is once again floating.

167. Save your work, and close InDesign.

Lesson 2 Review

Vocabulary

In a word processing document or on a sheet of paper, list all of the *key terms* in this lesson. Place each term on a separate line. Then, write a definition for each term using your own words. You will continue to build this terminology dictionary throughout this certification guide.

Review Questions

Answer the following questions. These questions are aligned to questions in the certification exam. Answering these questions will help prepare you to take the exam.

1. What items can be stored in an InDesign library?

   _____

   _____

   _____

2. Which option is set when creating a new document to create spreads with left- and right-hand pages?

   _____

3. What is the trim, and how is the trim shown in InDesign?

   _____

4. Describe how to add placeholder text to a text frame.

   _____

   _____

   _____

5. How is a tool in a flyout selected?

   _____

   _____

6. What are layers in InDesign?

   _____

   _____

7. Which button in the **Layers** panel is used to hide a layer?

   _____

8. What does clicking in the space to the right of the **Toggles visibility** button in the **Layers** panel do to the layer?

   _____

   _____

9. How do you rename Layer 2 to Circles?

   _____

   _____

   _____

   _____

10. Describe how to add page numbers to the bottom-center of a document.

_____

_____

_____

_____

11. How is a single page resized using the **Pages** panel?

_____

_____

_____

_____

12. How can a designer use the **Pages** panel to move a page to a different spread within the document?

_____

_____

_____

_____

13. How is a panel docked below another panel?

_____

_____

14. How can you remove a panel from the collapsed **Panels** bar and hide it?

_____

_____

_____

_____

15. When displayed, where are the rulers located?

_____

_____

Lesson 3
Color Models
and File Types

Objectives

Students will describe common color models. Students will explain color for printing. Students will classify images as raster or vector. Students will discuss sizing and resolution of digital images.

Color Models

Colors are defined using a *color model*, which is a way of mixing base colors to create a spectrum of colors. The RGB and CMYK color models are the most common color models used in graphic design. Other color models include hue, saturation, luminescence (HSL); hexadecimal; and L*A*B* color, as shown in **Figure 3-1.** The total spectrum of colors a given model can create is called the *gamut.*

Colors are assembled or blended using an additive or subtractive method. The *additive method* starts with no color, or black, and colors are added to create the final color. White in an additive color is the combination of all color wavelengths in light.

The *subtractive method* starts with all color, or white, and colors are removed to create the final color. For example, when you look at a red object, all color wavelengths in the light are absorbed by the paint (subtracted) except for red. What you see is the red wavelength. White is the reflection of all color wavelengths, so no color is subtracted. Black occurs when no color wavelengths are reflected, so all color is subtracted.

RGB

The name of the RGB color model comes from the three base colors used in the color model: red, green, and blue. All of the colors you see on a computer or television screen are made by mixing these three base colors.

RGB is an additive color model. Black is red 0, green 0, and blue 0. This means no color is added to the black screen. White is red 255, green 255, and blue 255. This means the maximum amount of all three colors is added to the black screen. All other colors are created on the screen by blending red, green, and blue in various values from 0 to 255.

CMYK

The name of the CMYK color model comes from the process colors used in commercial printing: cyan, magenta, and yellow. K stands for key color. The most detail in a printed image appears in the key color, which is almost always black.

Color Model	Features	Method
HSL (also known as HSB or HSV)	Creates color by a combination of hue, saturation, and luminescence (or brightness or value). This model is popular in creating textures and surfaces for 3D models. Since 3D models require the use of light and shadow to define position relative to the light source in the game, using this color model allows the computer to leave the hue and saturation of the texture unchanged while adjusting the luminescence setting to be brighter on the surface facing the light source and darker on the surface facing away from the light source.	Additive
RGB	Creates color by a combination of red, green, and blue. Blending these three colors allows for over 16 million colors at 8-bit depth.	Additive
RGBA	The RGB color model with support for alpha channels. Alpha channels are transparency channels. The alpha channel sets the saturation of an RGB color from full opacity (not see-through) to full transparency (completely see-through).	Additive
Hexadecimal	An RGB color model in which the color is represented as a series of six letters and numbers. This color model is used in web page design. Many imaging software programs allow the user to limit colors to "web only," which are 216 colors universally compatible with web browsers.	Additive
CMYK	Creates color by a combination of cyan, magenta, yellow, and a key color that is almost always black. This model is used for printed materials. Each of the colors corresponds to one of the four printing plates on a printing press.	Subtractive
L*A*B*	The description of the L*A*B* color model is a bit complicated as the L is for lightness and the A and B components are derived from a nonlinear color matrix, similar to an X,Y coordinate graph. This model seeks to create natural-looking colors. Additionally, L*A*B* color model is used to convert RGB color models to CMYK color models or vice versa. L*A*B* color works for both video displays (RGB) and printed materials (CMYK) and is considered device independent.	Matrix of both additive and subtractive combinations

Goodheart-Willcox Publisher

Figure 3-1.

A comparison of common color models.

Cyan, magenta, and yellow can be combined to create black, but the result tends to appear closer to dark brown than black when printed. By adding a key color of black, a "clean" black can be printed.

CMYK is a subtractive color model. Black is cyan 100%, magenta 100%, yellow 100%, and key 100%. This means 100% of each color is removed. White is cyan 0%, magenta 0%, yellow 0%, and key 0%. In practice, to create black in the CMYK color model, the settings are cyan 0%, magenta 0%, yellow 0%, and key 100%. This means the printer will lay down only black (the key color). Also in practice, to create white, the settings are cyan 0%, magenta 0%, yellow 0%, and key 0%. This means the printer will not lay down any color and the white paper color will show through.

HSL

The *hue, saturation, and luminescence (HSL)* color model, also known as the hue, saturation, and brightness (HSB) color model, creates color by adjusting these elements. Hue is the pigment color, saturation is how dark or rich the color is, and luminescence or brightness is how much light is shining on the color. This model is popular in creating textures and surfaces for 3D models. Since 3D models require the use of light and shadow to define position relative to the light source, using this color model allows the computer to leave the hue and saturation of the texture unchanged while adjusting the luminescence setting to be brighter on the surface facing the light source and darker on the surface facing away from the light source.

Hexadecimal Color

Hexadecimal color model is an RGB color model in which colors are represented by a series of six letters and numbers. For example, red in hexadecimal color is FF0000. The hexadecimal color model is used in web page design. Many imaging software programs allow the user to limit colors to "web only," which are 216 colors universally compatible with web browsers.

L*A*B*

The *L*A*B** color model seeks to create natural colors as the human eye would see them. The description of the L*A*B* color model is a bit complicated as the L is for lightness and the A and B components are derived from a nonlinear color matrix, similar to an X,Y coordinate graph. Additionally, the L*A*B* color model is used to convert RGB color models to CMYK color models or vice versa. L*A*B* color works for both video displays (RGB) and printed materials (CMYK) and is considered device independent.

Colors for Printing

Printed materials require different color inks to produce the colors on paper. As you learned earlier, the CMYK color model uses four colors of ink to create all of the other colors needed. A blended color used in printing is called a *process color.* In some instances, a color is needed that is not created by blending the four process colors (CMYK).

TIP

In industry, the CMYK color model is often referred to as simply *process color.*

A *spot color* is a premade color that is not mixed on the printer. The ink by itself provides the color. Some colors must be spot colors, like gold and silver. These colors contain special pigments and metal flakes that cannot be produced as a process color. In other cases, a printed item will only need a single color applied other than black. This is called two-color printing. For that printing, a spot color such as purple ink can be applied to the printed page where needed.

Monotone images are those images that use only one color of ink, such as black ink on white paper. A process called dithering is used to create shades of gray (or whatever color ink). *Halftoning* is spacing out the distance between the dots of color applied to the paper to create a blending of the ink and white paper, as shown in **Figure 3-2.** Printed items use halftoning to create gray with black ink. Halftoning is also used with four-color printing for reproducing photographs. Digital items use *grayscale* to lighten black to create gray.

Images

There are two basic types of images: raster and vector. All images created using a computer fall into one of these two categories. Additionally, digital images may be compressed to save storage space and reduce transmission times.

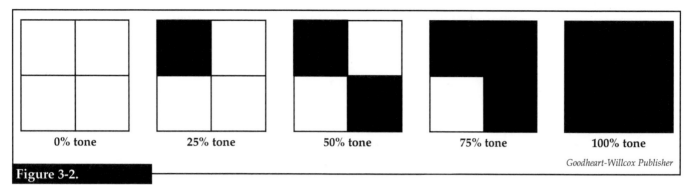

| 0% tone | 25% tone | 50% tone | 75% tone | 100% tone |

Goodheart-Willcox Publisher

Figure 3-2.

Shades of color are created in spot-color printing though halftoning or dithering.

Raster Images

Raster images are images made of dots or pixels. Each pixel in the image has a specific color and location to construct the final image. A raster image is called a *bitmap* because the location and color of each pixel is mapped. The computer reads a bitmap image by creating a coordinate grid with the origin at the top-left corner and increasing the X value moving right and the Y value moving down. In each space of the coordinate grid is a single pixel. A pixel can only be one color. To determine the color of a pixel at a particular coordinate location, the color value of a pixel is read by the computer and displayed.

Originally, bitmaps were only made at a bit depth of 1. *Bit depth* is a binary measurement for color. Binary allows for only two values, either a 1 or a 0. A bit depth of 1 describes the exponent value of the binary digit. A bit depth of 1 means 2^1. A bitmap value of 1 would, therefore, assign a white pixel on the coordinate grid where required. This produces a black-and-white image with no gray.

Eventually, computers were able to read bitmaps to a bit depth of 4. A bit depth of 4 allowed for a total of 16 colors, as 2^4 equals 16. The modern minimum standard for computer-displayed color is a bit depth of 8 or higher. A bit depth of 8, or 2^8, allows for 256 colors. Two hundred fifty-six–color devices are typically handheld devices where graphic quality is not needed. Computer monitors, HDTVs, and other devices that require quality graphics try to achieve true color or deep color.

True color has a bit depth of 24. True color uses the familiar RGB color model with 256 shades of red, 256 shades of green, and 256 shades of blue. True color produces 2^{24} colors, or 16,777,216 colors. Since the human eye is only capable of discriminating a little more than 10 million colors, 24-bit color can result in more colors than the human eye can see. Other color depths above 24 bit fall into the deep color range. *Deep color* is supported by Windows 7 and later up to a 48-bit depth. This provides more intense colors and shadow. Deep color can produce a gamut of over 1 billion colors.

Bit depth also allows for transparency. With a large gamut of color, an alpha channel can be allocated. The *alpha channel* varies the opacity of the color. The alpha channel can support from full transparency all the way to full opacity. A 16-bit alpha channel can support 65,536 values of transparency.

Alpha channels can also allow for a masking color. A *masking color* is a single shade of a color that can be set to be transparent. If you have ever seen a weather report on television, you have likely seen a masking color in use. Using a green or blue screen, called a chroma screen, will allow a background of the weather map to digitally replace the blank screen. In image creation, masking colors are typically chosen so they will not interfere with natural colors. Using a masking color such as white would be a very bad choice. If white were made to be transparent, then the white in a person's eyes and other white items would be transparent.

Vector Images

Vector images are images composed of lines, curves, and fills. Vector images do not store the color value and location of each pixel. Rather, the image is displayed based on the mathematical definition of each element in the image. In other words, in a raster image a line is composed of dots, while in a vector image the line is defined by a mathematical equation. For a vector image to be displayed, the software must rasterize the image before it is sent to the display device.

Some software programs can also convert raster images into vector images. This process is called *bitmap tracing.* The software will trace around zones that are the same or similar color to create a closed region and fill the region with a color.

A vector image can have a very small file size because the image is drawn by the computer using a mathematical formula. Since the formula draws the image, the image can be resized infinitely smaller or larger without loss of clarity, as shown in **Figure 3-3.** This is one of the biggest advantages of a vector image.

Goodheart-Willcox Publisher; image: Andreas Meyer/Shutterstock.com

Figure 3-3.

Raster images become pixelated when enlarged, but vector images can be infinitely scaled.

However, raster images offer an advantage over vector images because a vector image requires the CPU to work hard to draw the image. In the world of handheld devices with small CPUs and low memory, a vector image may have the benefit of a small file size, but may take up a large amount of CPU ability. Bitmaps do not take up a large amount of CPU ability, but have higher file size. The designer will need to understand the limits and capabilities of each device on which the image will be rendered to correctly match the file size and CPU usage to prevent lag and crashing the device.

Image File Compression

When working with images that are used on web pages or mobile devices, a designer should optimize the images. *Optimizing* an image is applying the most appropriate resolution and image file compression to achieve the smallest file size for the image quality needed. *Compression* uses mathematical formulas to approximate the location and color of each pixel and thereby reduce the total file size. Raster images are often compressed from their original raw format to reduce file size, save computer memory, and decrease download time.

A computer algorithm is used to record the pixel data in a smaller file size and then uncompress the image when it is opened in image-editing software. Almost all compression formats seek to eliminate the color values stored in the image that are beyond the capability of the human eye. The two most popular image-compression algorithms are lossy and lossless. The *lossy compression algorithm* compresses the image, but does not keep perfect image clarity. The image generally will have an acceptable appearance, but it will not be as clear when uncompressed as the original image. The *lossless compression algorithm,* or losslessly compression algorithm, compresses the image and keeps perfect clarity when uncompressed. There is a tradeoff between clarity and file size. To reduce the file size to run on a handheld device, the clarity may need to be reduced to fit the memory needs of the device and program.

File formats are needed for each type of compression so the computer will understand how to read the compressed image. **Figure 3-4** lists several popular image file formats and the compression model needed to expand the image.

Image Sizing and Resolution

When a bitmap image is enlarged, the existing pixels spread out. This *dithers* the image, which creates holes in the image where the pixels are no longer touching each other. Dithering is spacing out the distance between the dots of color applied to the paper or screen to create a blending of the color and the background. Dithering can also occur when color is undefined in the program such as a web browser.

Software uses a process called interpolation to dither an image. *Interpolation* is the refining of the space between pixels. During interpolation, the software averages the color of all pixels touching the empty space. The average color of the surrounding pixels is then assigned to the new pixel.

Part of optimizing a raster image is setting the proper resolution for the intended output. For example, an app for the iPad should have an icon that is 144 pixels × 144 pixels so the icon will properly display on the device and in the app store. A standard computer monitor has a resolution of 72 dots per inch (dpi) or 96 dpi. Making images for a website with a resolution higher than 96 dpi would not

File Format	Name	Image Type	Compression	Benefit
GIF	Graphic Interface Format	Raster	Lossless	Popular for use on websites; 256 colors and can be animated
PNG-8	Portable Network Graphic, 8-bit depth	Raster	Lossless	Same as GIF, but cannot be animated
PNG-24	Portable Network Graphic, 24-bit depth	Raster	Lossless	Same as PNG-8, but millions of colors and transparency options
JPEG	Joint Photographic Expert Group	Raster	Lossy	Generally offers the smallest file size
BMP	Bitmap	Raster	Run length encoded (RLE)	Device independent
TIFF	Tag Image File Format	Raster	Lossy and Lossless	Supported by most paint, imaging, and desktop publishing programs; not supported by many web browsers
RAW or CIFF	Camera Image File Format	Raster	None	Raw data at full uncompressed value obtained from a digital camera or scanner
SVG	Scalable Vector Graphic	Vector	Vector	Generic vector format that provides high resolution for print, web, and mobile devices; supported by most browsers and mobile devices; simple animated images are possible
AI	Adobe Illustrator	Vector	Vector	For use with Adobe Illustrator
EPS	Encapsulated PostScript	Vector	Vector	Generic vector format that can be used in any PostScript-enabled software; most commonly used for printing

Goodheart-Willcox Publisher

Figure 3-4.

Common file formats for graphics.

be properly optimizing the images. On the other hand, most images for print publication should be sized to specific dimensions with a resolution of 300 dpi.

The resolution of an image is measured in *dots per inch (dpi)* or *pixels per inch (ppi)*. This measure is the number of dots or pixels along the horizontal axis of an image multiplied by the number of dots or pixels along the vertical axis of the image. An image that is one inch square with 200 pixels on each axis has horizontal and vertical resolutions of 200 dpi. If this image is stretched to two inches square without resampling, the resolution becomes 100 dpi, which results in a loss of image clarity. If an image with a horizontal resolution of 200 dpi is 5 inches wide, the horizontal dimension contains 1000 pixels (5 inches × 200 dpi = 1000 pixels).

When an image is resized, it must be *resampled* to create a new image without reducing the image resolution. Resampling interpolates the image, adding or removing pixels as needed. Most imaging software gives the designer options for selecting a resampling method. A common resampling method is bicubic. There are two variations of bicubic resampling: bicubic for reduction and bicubic for enlargement. *Bicubic for reduction* is optimized for removing pixels, while *bicubic for enlargement* is optimized for creating pixels.

Lesson 3 Review

Vocabulary

In a word processing document or on a sheet of paper, list all of the *key terms* in this lesson. Place each term on a separate line. Then, write a definition for each term using your own words. You will continue to build this terminology dictionary throughout this certification guide.

Review Questions

Answer the following questions. These questions are aligned to questions in the certification exam. Answering these questions will help prepare you to take the exam.

1. What is a color called in printing that is created by blending CMYK inks?

   _____

2. Which color model would be best for an image that will be printed on a commercial printing press?

   _____

3. Which type of image is composed of lines, curves, and fills defined by mathematical equations?

   _____

4. Compare and contrast raster images with vector images.

   _____

   _____

   _____

   _____

5. Describe how an alpha channel and masking color control image transparency.

   _____

   _____

   _____

   _____

6. Describe bitmap tracing.

   _____

   _____

   _____

   _____

7. What are the two aspects of optimizing a raster image for use on a website or handheld device?

_____

_____

_____

_____

8. Which raster image file type supports millions of colors and transparency?

_____

9. Explain what happens when an image contains a color that is undefined in a web browser.

_____

_____

_____

_____

10. Which image file type is best for storing a simple vector animation?

_____

11. Which vector image file type is most commonly used for printing?

_____

12. Which image file type is best for photographs with lossy compression and generally offers the smallest file size?

_____

13. Which image file type is a lossless compression bitmap format for images used in printed materials such as a magazine, but is not supported by many web browsers?

_____

14. If the resolution of an image is 72 dpi and the image is 8 inches wide by 10 inches tall, how many pixels wide is the image?

_____

15. Which bicubic resampling method is best if enlarging an image from 300 pixels wide to 800 pixels wide?

_____

Lesson 4
Typography Activities

Objectives

Students will explain the function of frames in InDesign. Students will evaluate character spacing for kerning. Students will describe paths in InDesign. Students will place type on a path. Students will apply paragraph formatting. Students will explain the use of styles. Students will create columns for text in a document.

Situation

You are excelling in your apprentice program for layout artist. The company wants you to acquire new skills to increase your knowledge and to continue preparing for the Adobe Certified Associate (ACA) InDesign Creative Cloud industry certification exam. Your new task is to learn about typography and its use in InDesign.

How to Begin

1. Before beginning this lesson, download the needed files from the student companion website located at www.g-wlearning.com, and unzip them into your working folder.

2. Launch Adobe InDesign Creative Cloud.

3. Applying what you have learned, create a new document using the print intent. Set the page size to letter, and include two pages as a spread in the document.

4. Applying what you have learned, save the document as *LastName*_Dolphins in your working folder.

Frames

As you have seen, in InDesign, text is added to a text frame. Text, objects, and images are all added to a frame in InDesign. The frame is a container that holds the item.

5. Click the **Rectangle Frame Tool** button on the **Tools** panel.

6. Click and drag to draw a frame of any size on page 1.

7. Applying what you have learned, set the reference point for the text frame to its top-left corner. Before setting the X,Y coordinates for a frame, the correct reference point should be selected.

8. Applying what you have learned, enter 3p for the **X:** and **Y:** values for the frame. This positions the top-left corner of the frame from the top and left edges of the page. How many inches from these edges is the frame?

Rectangle Frame Tool

TIP
The origin (X=0, Y=0) for the page is the top-left corner of the page.

9. Applying what you have learned, change the width of the text frame to 45p and the height to 9p. How many inches wide and high is the frame?

_____

Type Tool

10. Click the **Type Tool** button in the **Tools** panel, and click the frame. The frame is converted to a text frame. Text can now be added to the frame. Notice the options available in the **Control** panel when the **Type Tool** is selected.

11. Add the text Dolphin Tours and More to the frame.

12. With the **Type Tool** active, click and drag over the text in the frame to select it. The text is highlighted, as shown in **Figure 4-1.**

Character Formatting Controls

13. In the **Control** panel, click the **Character Formatting Controls** button so it is on (depressed or gray). This will display options to change the style of letters and other characters.

14. Click the typeface drop-down arrow, and click **Elephant** in the drop-down list. If this typeface is not installed on your computer, select any serif typeface.

15. Click in the **Font Size** text box, and enter 48 pt.

Small Caps

16. Click the **Small Caps** button. This changes the lowercase letters to uppercase letters that are smaller than the normal uppercase letters.

17. Click in the **Tracking** text box, and enter –10. A negative value pushes the letters closer together by reducing the spacing between characters. Remember, tracking adjusts the spacing between all characters.

TIP

Below the **Character Formatting Controls** button is the **Paragraph Formatting Controls** button. This will change the **Control** panel to display options to adjust paragraph alignment and styles.

18. Click the down arrow for **Horizontal Scale** until all of the text fits on one line. Changing the horizontal scale stretches or shrinks each character's width.

19. Click in the **Vertical Scale** text box, and enter 125%. Adjusting the vertical scale stretches or shrinks each character's height.

20. Click after the E in the word *More* to position the text insertion point there, then press the [Enter] key to begin a new line of text. Pressing the [Enter] key creates a *hard return,* which forces text to begin on a new line.

21. On the second line, add the text Interactive Adventures.

22. Applying what you have learned, adjust the horizontal scale of the text on the second line so it stretches across the entire width of the text frame.

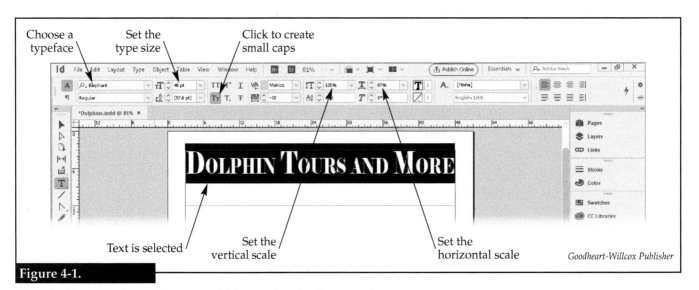

Goodheart-Willcox Publisher

Figure 4-1.
Use the **Type Tool** to select text, which can then be formatted.

23. With *Interactive Adventures* selected, click in the **Baseline Shift** text box, and enter 13 pt. The text is moved upward and almost touches the first line of text, as shown in **Figure 4-2.**

Kerning

As you learned earlier, kerning adjusts the spacing between character pairs to create overlap. Most letters and other characters fill up a rectangular space and are placed next to each other. Some characters need to overlap to look like there is the correct spacing between them.

24. Applying what you have learned, select the DV letter pair in the word *Adventures*. Notice how there appears to be too much of a gap between these letters.

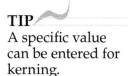

TIP
A specific value can be entered for kerning.

25. Click the **Kerning** drop-down arrow on the **Control** panel, and click **Optical** in the drop-down list. Notice how the gap between the DV letter pair is reduced.

26. Applying what you have learned, set the kerning to optical for the AC letter pair in the word *Interactive*, the OL letter pair in *Dolphin*, the OU letter pair in *Tours*, and the MO letter pair in *More*.

27. Click between the PH letter pair in *Dolphin*. Notice that the kerning value is 0.

28. Click between the AC letter pair in the word *Interactive*. Notice that the kerning value is –46.

29. Applying what you have learned, adjust the horizontal scale of each line of text so it fills the frame.

Path

When creating a line or shape, InDesign draws an invisible *path* on the document in the shape of the line or outline of a shape. The path can later have a stroke applied to it to give it thickness, design, and color.

30. Click the **Line Tool** button on the **Tools** panel.

Line Tool

31. Click below the second line of text, hold down the [Shift] key, and drag to draw a path across the page from page edge to page edge, as shown in **Figure 4-3.** The path can extend past the edge of the page as anything beyond the trim will not print. Holding down the [Shift] key limits the line to 45-degree angles (0, 45, 90, etc.).

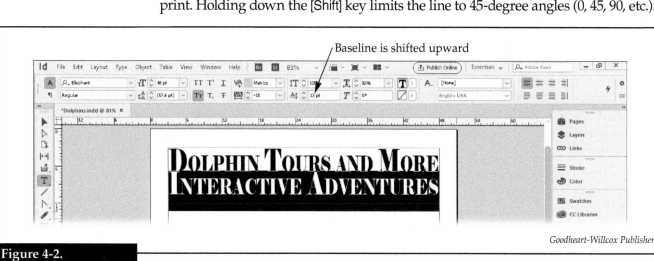

Goodheart-Willcox Publisher

Figure 4-2.

Shifting the baseline moves the characters either up or down on the page.

Path is drawn

Anything beyond the trim will not print

Goodheart-Willcox Publisher

Figure 4-3.

Drawing a path across the page. Hold down the [Shift] key to constrain the path to 45-degree angles.

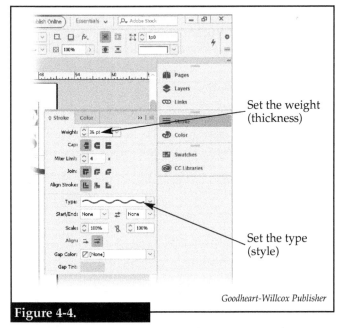

Set the weight (thickness)

Set the type (style)

Goodheart-Willcox Publisher

Figure 4-4.

The stroke is formatted using the **Stroke** panel. Formatting options can also be found on the **Control** panel.

32. With the path selected, click the **Stroke** panel in the **Panels** bar to expand it, as shown in **Figure 4-4.** The *stroke* is the line applied to the path.

33. Click in the **Weight:** text box, and enter 36 pt. The weight is the thickness of the stroke. A higher value for weight makes a thicker line.

34. Click the **Type:** drop-down arrow, and click **Wavy** in the drop-down list. The type for a stroke is the style of the line.

35. Applying what you have learned, change the stroke color to dark blue (C100, M90, Y10, K0).

36. Collapse the **Stroke** panel.

37. Using the **Selection Tool**, drag the line upward until it is aligned with the bottom of the text frame. Use smart guides to help with alignment.

38. Applying what you have learned, copy and paste the line. Then, move the copy below the original so the top of the copy is aligned with the bottom of the original.

Type on a Path

A creative means of adding design to a document is to make type follow a path. In this manner, text can be made to appear in a circle, wavy line, rectangle, or other shape.

39. Zoom in so the page width fills the document window. This will make it easier to see the path as you are drawing it.

40. Click the **Pencil Tool** button on the **Tools** panel. This tool is used to draw a freehand path, such as a wavy path between the two wavy lines.

41. Click and hold where the bottom wavy line and the left margin intersect. While holding the mouse button, drag to the right to draw a line that follows the wavy line to the right margin, as shown in **Figure 4-5.** If you are not happy with the path, press the [Ctrl][Z] key combination to undo the drawing. Then, use the **Pencil Tool** and try again.

TIP

To quickly zoom, press the [Ctrl][+] key combination ([Command Key][+] on a Mac) to zoom in or [Ctrl][–] to zoom out.

Pencil Tool

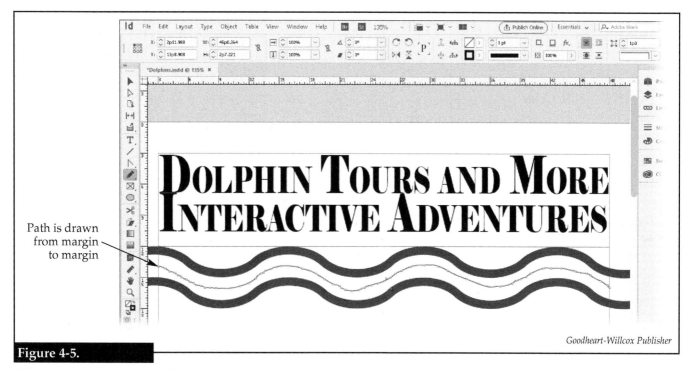

Path is drawn from margin to margin

Goodheart-Willcox Publisher

Figure 4-5.

The **Pencil Tool** is used to draw a freehand path.

TIP

When using the **Type on a Path Tool**, the cursor will display a plus sign (+) when it is over a valid path on which text can be placed.

Type on a Path Tool

Paragraph Formatting Controls

Align center

A

Character Formatting Controls

42. With the path selected, use the arrow keys on the keyboard to move the path between the two wavy lines.

43. Applying what you have learned, change the stroke color of the path to red, the weight to 6 points, and the type to solid.

44. Click the **Type on a Path Tool** button on the **Tools** panel.

45. Click at the left end of the red wavy line path, and add this text: Swim with the Dolphins Adventure is Available NOW!

Paragraph Formatting

As you have seen, when text is selected, the **Control** panel can display character-formatting options. Character formatting is limited to customizing the look and spacing of the letters and other characters. Options for formatting the paragraph can also be displayed in the **Control** panel. This formatting is limited to changes that affect the entire paragraph, such as shape and alignment.

46. Applying what you have learned, select the text on the path. Either the **Type Tool** or **Type on a Path** tool can be used to select the text.

47. Click the **Paragraph Formatting Controls** button on the **Control** panel. Options for changing the paragraph formatting are displayed in the **Control** panel.

48. Click the **Align center** button. The text is moved to the center of the path.

49. Applying what you have learned, display the character formatting options in the **Control** panel.

50. Applying what you have learned, change the typeface to Brush Script MT and the size to 36 points. If this typeface is not installed on your computer, select any decorative, script typeface.

51. Change to the **Selection Tool**. The path should be automatically selected. If not, click the red line to select the path.

52. Applying what you have learned, change the stroke color to None. The path is hidden, and its weight is set to 0, as shown in **Figure 4-6.**

53. Use the arrow keys to move the path so the text is vertically centered between the wavy lines.

54. Applying what you have learned, select the text on the path, and change the color to cyan with a black outline.

Paragraph Styles

A *style* is a saved group of formatting settings that can be applied in one step. Styles are used to keep formatting consistent throughout a document. There are character styles and paragraph styles in InDesign.

55. Click **Type>Paragraph Styles** on the **Application** bar. The **Paragraph Styles** panel is displayed in a floating position. This is actually a panel group, and it also contains the **Character Styles** panel.

56. Dock the panel group at the bottom of the **Panels** bar, and expand the **Paragraph Styles** panel.

57. Applying what you have learned, select the type on the path.

58. Click the **Create New Style** button at the bottom of the **Paragraph Styles** panel. A new style named Paragraph Style 1 is added to the panel.

59. Right-click on the new style (Paragraph Style 1) in the **Paragraph Styles** panel, and click **Edit "Paragraph Style 1"...** in the shortcut menu. The **Paragraph Style Options** dialog box is displayed, as shown in **Figure 4-7.**

60. Click **General** on the left side of the dialog box. Then, click in the **Style Name:** text box and change the name to Blue Script.

61. Click **Basic Character Formats** on the left side of the dialog box. Notice the text formatting properties match those of the selected text. Also examine the properties in the **Character Color** category.

62. Click the **OK** button to save the changes to the style.

TIP
By selecting text before creating a new style, the new style will automatically have the properties of the selected text.

Create New Style

TIP
Manually modifying type from the base settings of a style is called a *style override.* Generally, overrides should be avoided.

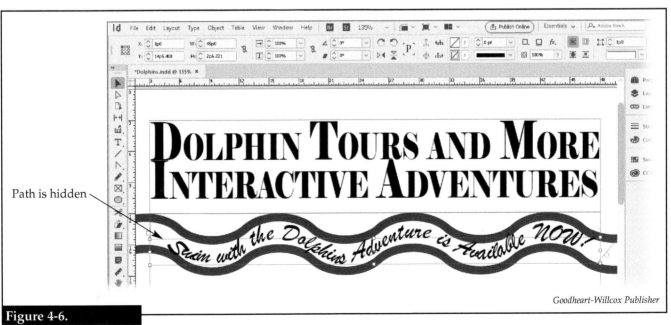

Path is hidden

Goodheart-Willcox Publisher

Figure 4-6.

By changing the stroke color to None, the path is hidden and its weight is set to 0.

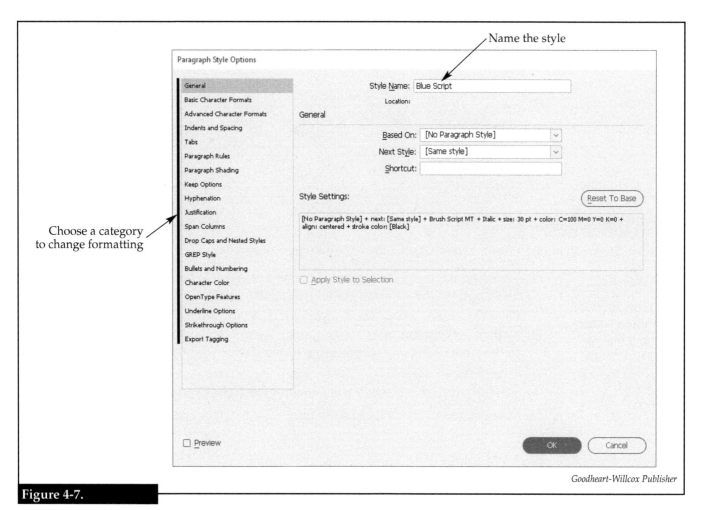

Goodheart-Willcox Publisher

Figure 4-7.

Defining the properties for a paragraph style.

63. With the type on the path selected, click the Blue Script style in the **Paragraph Styles** panel. This applies the style to the selected text. Previously, the text had been modified from the default settings. By applying the style, even though there is no visible change in the type, the paragraph conforms to the style settings.

Columns

As you saw in a previous lesson, columns can be set up when the document is created. Columns can also be set up at any time. Columns provide guides for the designer to align text frames.

64. Click **Layout>Margins and Columns…** on the **Application** bar. The **Margins and Columns** dialog box is displayed, as shown in **Figure 4-8**.

65. In the **Columns** area, click in the **Number:** text box, and enter 2. This will create guides for two columns on the page.

66. Click in the **Gutter:** text box, and enter 0.25 in. This is the distance between the columns. How much space is between the columns as measured in picas and points?

67. Click the **OK** button to apply the columns. Notice that there are more pink guidelines to show where the columns can be drawn.

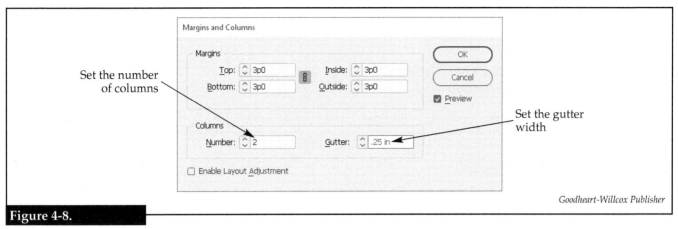

Set the number of columns

Set the gutter width

Goodheart-Willcox Publisher

Figure 4-8.

Adding columns to the document, and setting the distance between columns.

TIP
The **Type Tool** only draws text frames. It cannot be used to draw a frame for other types of objects.

68. Applying what you have learned, draw a text frame below the wavy lines that fills the area from left margin to first column guide and down to the bottom margin.

69. Applying what you have learned, drag the top-center handle of the text frame so the frame extends to the bottom of the lowest wavy line. Use smart guides to assist you.

70. Similarly, create and size a text frame in the right-hand column.

71. Save your work, and close InDesign.

Lesson 4 Review

Vocabulary

In a word processing document or on a sheet of paper, list all of the *key terms* in this lesson. Place each term on a separate line. Then, write a definition for each term using your own words. You will continue to build this terminology dictionary throughout this certification guide.

Review Questions

Answer the following questions. These questions are aligned to questions in the certification exam. Answering these questions will help prepare you to take the exam.

1. Briefly describe how to convert a rectangular frame into a text frame.

_____

_____

_____

_____

2. What are the two different modes for the **Control** panel when type is selected (what are the names of the buttons)?

_____

3. What are small caps?

_____

_____

4. Which property controls the width of characters without affecting their height?

_____

5. How can characters be adjusted so they are taller without changing their width?

_____

_____

6. Which property in InDesign controls the position of the invisible line on which type is placed?

_____

7. Where in InDesign can you change the kerning and tracking?

_____

8. Which InDesign panel allows a designer to change a line from straight to wavy?

_____

9. When dragging a text frame, what helper feature of InDesign helps the designer align the top of the frame to the bottom of another text frame?

_____

10. Which tool allows a freehand path to be drawn?

_____

11. Briefly describe how to make type follow a path in InDesign.

_____

_____

_____

_____

12. How is a new paragraph style created?

_____

13. What is the benefit of selecting text before creating a new paragraph style?

_____

_____

14. How is a paragraph style applied to selected text?

_____

15. Briefly describe how to add column guides to a document after the document has been created.

_____

_____

_____

_____

Lesson 5
Digital Project Management

Objectives

Students will evaluate the preproduction stage of production for a digital media project. Students will describe conversion of traditional artwork and photographs into digital assets. Students will compare and contrast hard and soft proofs. Students will discuss collaboration and sharing of assets.

Reading Materials

A designer using InDesign should apply client-centric design principles. *Client-centric design* simply means that the needs and wants of the client are used to create the work. This requires significant communication with the client to discover exactly what he or she expects the final product to look like and how it will perform. Designers should avoid pushing their own style preferences and instead focus on the client, target audience, and industry standards.

A design project will follow a path through four stages of production. The stages are: preproduction, production, testing, and publication, as shown in **Figure 5-1.**

Project Stage	Activities
Preproduction	Client interview; target-market analysis; sketches or storyboards to summarize planning and analysis
Production	Refine sketches; design; build
Testing	Performance test on technology devices being used; market testing with target-market subjects to align to client goals
Publication	Final revisions from testing results implemented; publish for public use

Goodheart-Willcox Publisher

Figure 5-1.

The four stages of production for a design project.

Preproduction

The preproduction stage is the most important stage of production. The preproduction stage involves gathering information and planning out how the job will get done. During preproduction, the project manager will interview the client, conduct research, and gather customer demographic information to best determine what project requirements need to be met. Afterward, the project manager is responsible for:

- selecting the best team members for the job;
- identifying the tasks; and
- determining deadlines for the project.

Preproduction Interviews

The *client* is the person requesting the work. When working with a client, it is important to have a full understanding of what he or she expects. You should conduct *preproduction interviews* with the client to brainstorm ideas and fully communicate the goals for the finished product. A preproduction interview occurs *before* any work begins. If you start working without this important step, the client may be dissatisfied with the result, and you will have to redo the project. In the professional world, you are paid by the client, and the client will not pay for unsatisfactory work that does not meet the specified goals. Working with the client in a preproduction interview, you will need to identify the client goals and target market. These are the two basic criteria that will guide the project.

The *client goals* set the direction of the creative work. The client is paying you to create something to meet a goal, often attracting customers. This means the graphics and layout need to meet these goals, or the client will feel he or she did not receive the service for which payment was made. Client goals can include what the graphics will be used for, such as packaging, website, billboard, employee handbook, etc., and the specifications for graphics. The specifications for an image used on a billboard will be much different from those for an image used on a website. Additionally, the client may have goals of informing or attracting attention. The use of color is important in attracting attention, while color in informational items may have little value.

The *target market* is a group of people for whom the work is intended. The target market for a comic book–style layout is likely very different from the target market for a traditional annual report. If the target market is children, an advertising project may have little or no text, may contain fantasy characters, and may use bright colors. If the audience is college graduates, the advertisement may contain large blocks of text and photorealistic images or photographs. Use surveys and interviews to test the appeal of the design to members of the target market who will be using the product.

A target market is defined by demographics. *Demographics* are shared traits of a group. The demographics of a high school class might include age, achievement, and geographic location. The students in a single 11th-grade class might all be 15–17 years old, passed the 10th grade, and live within three miles of the school. It is important to understand the demographics because demographics help segment a population of people into smaller groups that have similar characteristics. The similarities allow the designer to create items that will appeal to that specific target audience and not everyone in the population.

Preproduction Deliverables and Communication

Before starting to build a layout in InDesign, preproduction deliverables should be defined and created. These should be communicated to the client along with any other information that is relevant to the project.

Preproduction deliverables include sketches and specifications. From the client interviews, you can work out the use of the layout and find out the quality needed for images and graphics. *Sketching* the design is always a great way to show the client that you understand what he or she wants and how to create the finished product. *Specifications* include the scope of the work to be done and the deadline. The *deadline* is the date the project must be delivered to the client.

Scope defines how the layout will be output in final form and the intended use. Is the layout going to go on a web page, or is it going to be on a roadside billboard? The difference between these final forms greatly affects the way the digital design work is done. The documentation of a project's scope, which is called a *scope statement, scope of project document,* or *statement of work,* explains the boundaries of the project and establishes responsibilities for each team member. During the project, this documentation helps the team remain focused and on task. The scope statement also provides the project team with guidelines for making decisions about change requests during the project. Having a clear scope statement will help prevent scope creep. *Scope creep* is the uncontrolled changes or additions to the project's scope. Scope creep can cause huge delays and cost overruns.

Part of the scope is a definition of the formality of the project. *Formality* is the degree to which something follows an accepted set of rules. Events have varying degrees of formality. A wedding is often very formal—it has high formality—with an elaborate production of wedding gowns, tuxedos, limousines, and more. However, a wedding may be very informal—it has low formality—with just the bride and groom wearing flip-flops and swimsuits in a small ceremony at the beach. The designer of a wedding invitation for these weddings needs to know how formal or informal to make the design. Products such as restaurant menus need to match the formality of the location. Formality must match the client goals, purpose of the document, and the target market needs for the design to be effective.

Preproduction deliverables enhance the communication and understanding between the client and design team. The design team will be responsible for keeping the client informed and part of the process throughout every stage of the design project. Use the following best practices to help achieve a successful relationship with the client.

- During preproduction, use sketches and mockups to help the client visualize the designs you are planning to create.
- To track the changes and approval of the client, the designer should make notes on the sketches and have the client approve the basic design by signing the sketches. This creates a record of the client's approval for any changes to the project.
- Updating the client on the overall progress and getting approval on any completed artwork limits the chances of having problems at the end.

Before the preproduction phase ends, the designer should have a firm understanding of what the client wants and the design elements that need to be created.

Conversion of Traditional Artwork and Printed Photographs

The digital artist may need to perform a *conversion* to change physical art into digital format, or to *digitize* the artwork. Typically, conversions are performed on traditional output such as drawings, paintings, and continuous tone (nondigital) photographs. When performing these conversions, the most important consideration is the technology needed to properly convert the image to the best quality of digital image for the application. A sketch may simply need to be photographed by a digital camera to make it a digital sketch. A digital camera takes a photograph, but in digital form instead of on film. A high-quality painting might need a digital scanner to capture the quality of the image. A digital scanner passes light over an image, similar to how a photocopy machine works, and digitally records each point of color. A digital camera or scanner creates a raster image when it records each point of color. Other items that may need to be converted into digital format are photographic slides or other nonstandard images. *Slides* are photographs printed on transparent film from which the image is projected onto a screen to view it. Special equipment is often needed to properly transfer slides to digital format.

Whenever possible, have the client submit the images in digital format so you do not have to do the conversions. This will save you time and also place the responsibility for the quality of the conversion on the client. The client can also save money by not having to pay you to do the conversions. However, in many cases the client will not have the ability to do the conversion or the technical knowledge to provide the proper quality.

Proofs

Before creating the final images in all the required formats, the client should review and approve the work. The output you provide the client is a proof. A *proof* is a copy of the final output created for approval. When the client signs off on a proof, he or she is giving approval to create the final output needed. A *hard proof* is a physical proof printed on paper or various other substrates, while a *soft proof* is viewed on the computer. Adobe InDesign offers a soft-proof mode to simulate how a printed image will be rendered when output. Using the Working CMYK or Document CMYK proof setup will convert the printable CMYK color model into the video RGB color model displayed on the computer monitor. To toggle soft-proof mode, click **View>Proof Colors** on the **Application** bar.

An advantage of a soft proof or electronic proof over a hard proof is the ability to quickly see how the image would look in different outputs. Changing color models or output devices will change the overall look of the layout in the soft proof. To do the same thing with a hard proof, a new proof would have to be pulled for each version. Soft proofs are also a cost-saving device, as hard proofs can be expensive to generate.

Collaboration and Sharing Assets

Many times, you will collaborate with other designers during a project. Using the Adobe Creative Cloud and Adobe Bridge will help organize and share work. *Adobe Creative Cloud* offers a way to share files, give feedback, and save settings across devices. *Adobe Bridge* or, in CS6, the **Mini Bridge** tab provides a convenient portal to store design elements, such as images, used in more than one Adobe program. For example, an image altered in Adobe Illustrator will be used in Adobe InDesign to create a layout. Adobe Bridge allows the image to be placed in the InDesign layout. The artist can use Illustrator to manipulate the image and resave it in Adobe Bridge. The image will automatically update in the InDesign layout. Adobe Bridge provides a convenient way to manage, open, and view design assets and files.

Adobe Bridge allows an image file to be linked from one program to another. *Linking* maintains a connection to the original image file. If the image file is updated in the source program, it is automatically updated in the shared program. If the image is *embedded*, however, it is a copy of the image without a connection to the original file. Altering the original image file does not automatically update the image in the shared program. In order to update the image in the shared program, the existing image must be manually replaced with the updated image.

Lesson 5 Review

Vocabulary

In a word processing document or on a sheet of paper, list all of the *key terms* in this lesson. Place each term on a separate line. Then, write a definition for each term using your own words. You will continue to build this terminology dictionary throughout this certification guide.

Review Questions

Answer the following questions. These questions are aligned to questions in the certification exam. Answering these questions will help prepare you to take the exam.

1. Which type of design principles should a designer focus on instead of pushing his or her own design style preferences, and what is the focus of these principles?

2. List the four stages of the project development process in the correct order.

3. What are three responsibilities of a project manager during preproduction?

4. What two criteria should guide the digital artist when creating art for a client?

5. What are three techniques that may be used in creating an advertisement for children?

6. What can a designer use to test the appeal of a design to the target market?

7. Why does a designer need to understand the demographics of the target audience?

_____

_____

_____

8. What is the term for the date when a project must be completed and delivered to the client?

_____

9. What problem related to project management can occur if the scope is not properly defined?

_____

10. Which level of formality would you expect a menu from a drive-through restaurant to have? Explain your answer using specific details that support your claim.

_____

_____

_____

_____

11. List three best practices to make sure the project meets the client's needs.

_____

_____

_____

_____

_____

_____

12. Images produced with a scanner or digital camera are which type of image? Why?

_____

_____

_____

13. Which viewing mode in InDesign is best for viewing on a computer monitor for a layout that will be printed?

_____

14. Which two features in Adobe InDesign allow sharing of art assets between other Adobe programs?

_____

_____

15. What is the difference between a linked image and an embedded image?

_____

_____

_____

Lesson 6
Layout and Styles

Objectives

Students will explain the process of threading text between frames. Students will apply character and paragraph formatting. Students will create paragraph and character styles. Students will identify a drop cap. Students will create unassigned frames. Students will explain how to place and resize an image in a frame. Students will describe captions. Students will discuss the process of changing an image link. Students will export a document to a PDF file.

How to Begin

InDesign is a layout program that will allow you to quickly add content from other sources and make it look great. The client wants to reuse the contents from his website for this document.

1. Before beginning this lesson, download the needed files from the student companion website located at www.g-wlearning.com, and unzip them into your working folder.

2. Launch your computer's file explorer, display it as a window (not full screen), and leave it open.

3. Launch Adobe InDesign Creative Cloud.

4. On the opening screen or splash page, click the thumbnail for the *LastName*_Dolphins file. If this file is not listed or the splash page is not displayed, click **File>Open...**, navigate to your working folder, and open the file.

5. Switch to your system's file explorer, navigate to your working folder, select the Lesson06_Main Article.rtf file, and drag and drop it into the text frame for the left column in InDesign, as shown in **Figure 6-1.** The text from the file automatically fills the column. Notice the red square and plus sign at the bottom of the column. This means there is more text in the frame than can be displayed at the frame's current size.

Threading Text

When there is more text than will fit into a text frame, the text that cannot be seen is called *overset text.* Text frames can be linked so overflow text from one frame automatically flows into the other frame. This is called *text threading.* The frame that contains too much text has an *outport* that is threaded to the *inport* of the frame that will accept the overset text. InDesign can create threaded connections from outports to inports to link several text frames across several pages if needed. In this case, you will be using the right column to handle the overset text that does not fit in the left column.

6. Locate the red square near the bottom-right corner of the text frame in the left column. This icon indicates overset text.

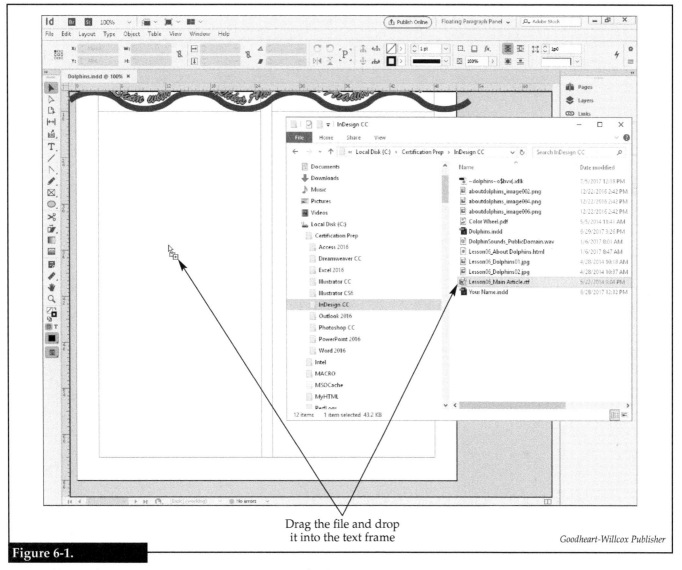

Drag the file and drop
it into the text frame

Goodheart-Willcox Publisher

Figure 6-1.

A text file can be dragged and dropped into a text frame in InDesign.

Selection Tool

7. Click the **Selection Tool**, and then click the overset icon. The icon changes to a right-pointing arrow, which is the outport icon, as shown in **Figure 6-2.** The cursor also changes to a standard arrow cursor. These indicate the text is ready to be threaded into a new frame.

8. Click the text frame in the right column. The overset text automatically flows into the frame. Notice the inport icon at the top of the text frame in the right column. Also notice there is no outport icon on this text frame because there is no overset text.

Character and Paragraph Formatting

9. Applying what you have learned, select the first heading in the article, *Dolphins in the Wild*, and display the character-formatting options in the **Control** panel.

10. Change the typeface to Book Antiqua or other serif typeface and the type size to 20 points.

Fill

11. Click the drop-down arrow next to the **Fill** button on the **Control** panel. Notice a new color swatch has been added based on the color of the text in the file that

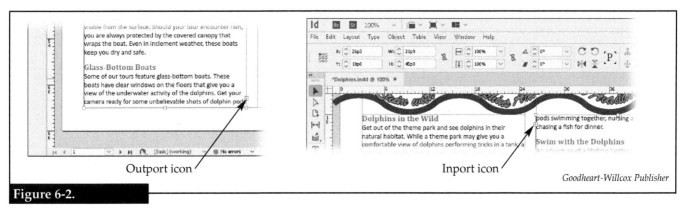

Outport icon

Inport icon

Goodheart-Willcox Publisher

Figure 6-2.

Overset text can be threaded from one text frame to another.

was loaded. This new color is named RTF r79 g129 b189, which indicates it came from an RTF file and provides the RGB values of the color.

12. Double-click the RTF r79 g129 b189 swatch to open the **Swatch Options** dialog box.

13. Uncheck the **Name with Color Value** check box, and change the name of the color to Medium Blue.

14. Applying what you have learned, set the color type to process color and the color mode to CMYK.

15. Change the color values to C100, M75, Y10, and K0. Then, click the **OK** button to update the color. Editing the color imported from the RTF file will affect all heads in the imported file as they all share the same color.

Stroke

16. Click the drop-down arrow next to the **Stroke** button on the **Control** panel, and in the drop-down panel that is displayed, change the color to Paper. This applies a white outline around each letter. For the most part, this effect will not be visible, but if any letter crosses the wavy line above, this white outline will provide contrast so the letter is fully visible.

Paragraph Formatting Controls

17. Applying what you have learned, display the paragraph-formatting options in the **Control** panel.

18. Click the **Align center** button on the **Control** panel to center the selected text.

Align center

Paragraph and Character Styles

Remember, manually altering the formatting of selected text instead of editing the style is a style override. Generally, style overrides should be avoided. However, overriding a style is an easy way to create the foundation for creating a new style. Use of styles ensures similar items in the document will all have the same treatment.

19. Be sure the paragraph-formatting controls are displayed in the **Control** panel.

Paragraph Style

20. With the *Dolphins in the Wild* text selected, click the **Paragraph Style** button, and click **New Paragraph Style…** in the drop-down list, as shown in **Figure 6-3**. The **New Paragraph Style** dialog box is displayed. This dialog box is the same as the **Paragraph Style Options** dialog box discussed earlier. Notice that all the formatting applied as a style override is automatically filled in.

21. Applying what you have learned, change the style name to Section Headings.

22. Click **General** on the left, click the **Based On:** drop-down arrow, and click **No Paragraph Style** in the list. This removes any connection to the previous style

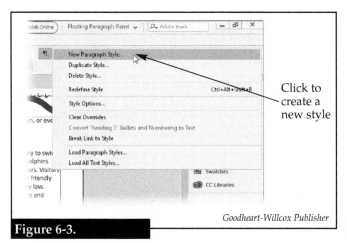

Click to create a new style

Goodheart-Willcox Publisher

Figure 6-3.

Click the **Paragraph Style** button to display a drop-down menu.

(heading 2), but retains the formatting of the style and the manual overrides. Click the **OK** button to create the new style based on the formatting of the selected text.

23. Applying what you have learned, apply the new style to all four headings in the imported text.

24. Applying what you have learned, create a new character fill color swatch named Light Blue with CMYK color of C50, M25, Y0, and K0.

25. Select the text on the path, and apply the Light Blue color to it.

26. Click **Window>Styles>Character Styles** on the **Application** bar to display the **Character Styles** panel. A character style is created in the same basic way as a paragraph style is created.

27. Applying what you have learned, create a new character style named Light Blue Chars. In the **Character Style Options** dialog box, click **Character Color** on the left, and assign the Light Blue color to the character style.

28. Applying what you have learned, assign the new Light Blue Chars character style to the title text *Dolphin Tours and More Interactive Adventures.*

Drop Cap

A drop cap is a typographical style in which the first letter of a paragraph is enlarged and extends down into the second line of text, as shown in **Figure 6-4.** The size of a drop cap determines how many lines of text it extends downward.

Normal

Drop cap

Goodheart-Willcox Publisher

Figure 6-4.

A drop cap is a stylistic treatment for text.

TIP

The up and down arrows next to the text boxes can be used to increase or decrease the value in increments of 1.

TIP

The best practice is to create a new paragraph style for the paragraphs containing drop caps to ensure consistency throughout the document. However, in a short, one-page document, manually applying the formatting may be acceptable.

TIP

Some text wrap settings can be changed in the **Control** panel when a frame is selected, but only general settings are available. Use the panel for access to all available text wrap features.

Jump object

29. Applying what you have learned, select just the G in the word *Get* in the first paragraph below the head *Dolphins in the Wild*.

30. Applying what you have learned, change the typeface to Broadway or another serif typeface.

31. With the **Type Tool** active, click anywhere in the first paragraph. A drop cap is a paragraph-formatting feature, so text does not need to be selected, but the insertion point must be within the paragraph that will have the drop cap.

32. Applying what you have learned, display the paragraph formatting controls in the **Control** panel.

33. Click in the **Drop Cap Number of Lines** text box, and enter 3, as shown in **Figure 6-5**. This enlarges the G to fill three lines of text.

34. Click in the **Drop Cap One or More Characters** text box, and enter 7. This includes the first seven characters of the paragraph as part of the drop cap.

35. Applying what you have learned, modify the drop cap settings so only the first letter (G) is included and it spans two vertical lines.

36. Applying what you have learned, format the first paragraph below each heading to match the drop cap you just created.

Unassigned Frames and Text Wrapping

There are three types of frames in InDesign: text, graphic, and unassigned. Frames drawn with the **Rectangle Frame Tool**, **Ellipse Frame Tool**, and **Polygon Frame Tool** are typically unassigned frames. These frames can later be filled with either text or graphics. To have type flow around a frame, text wrapping is set.

37. Applying what you have learned, use the **Rectangle Frame Tool** to draw a frame that fits in the left column under the heading *Dolphins in the Wild*. Notice the frame is on top of the text as it has not been set to wrap text.

38. Applying what you have learned, set the reference point to the top-left corner, X location to 0.5 in, Y location to 4 in, width to 3.625 in, and height to 2.0 in. What is the width and height of the frame in picas and points?

_____

39. Click **Window>Text Wrap** on the **Application** bar to display the **Text Wrap** panel.

40. Hover the cursor over each of the buttons at the top of the **Text Wrap** panel to display the help text. These buttons control how text wraps around the frame. Click the **Jump object** button. Notice how the text jumps around the object and continues below it, as shown in **Figure 6-6**.

Enter the number of vertical lines for the drop cap

Enter the number of characters to include

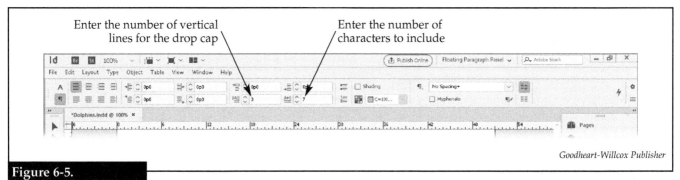

Goodheart-Willcox Publisher

Figure 6-5.

Creating a drop cap, which is a paragraph-formatting feature.

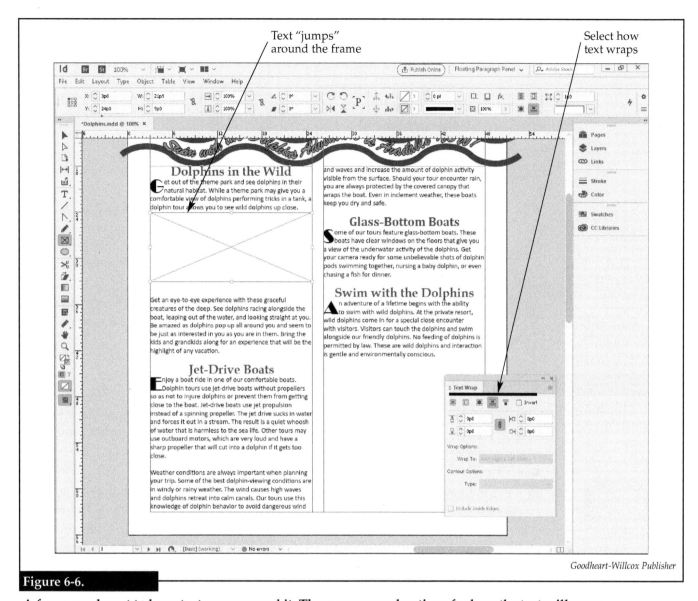

Text "jumps" around the frame

Select how text wraps

Goodheart-Willcox Publisher

Figure 6-6.

A frame can be set to have text wrap around it. There are several options for how the text will wrap.

Adding Images to Frames

An image can be added to either an unassigned frame or a closed drawing shape, such as a rectangle or ellipse. In this case, you will be adding a linked image to the unassigned frame. Recall, a linked image maintains a connection to the original file. If the image file is later changed, the frame can be updated to the new image.

41. Without anything selected, click **File>Place…** on the **Application** bar. A standard open-type dialog box is displayed.

42. Navigate to your working folder, select the Lesson06_Dolphins01.jpg image file, and click the **Open** button.

43. Click the unassigned frame to place the image in the frame, which converts the unassigned frame to a graphic frame. It may look like part of the image is cut off. That is because the image is larger than the frame.

TIP
If a frame is selected before clicking **File>Place…**, the image will be automatically inserted into the selected frame.

Content indicator

Image is shifted up and right

Figure 6-7.

Goodheart-Willcox Publisher

Clicking the content indicator allows the image to be shifted within the frame.

44. Activate the **Selection Tool**, and move the cursor over the frame. Notice two faint, concentric circles are displayed in the middle of the frame, as shown in **Figure 6-7.** This is the content indicator. It is used to shift the content around within the frame.

45. Click the content indicator. An orange bounding box appears surrounding the entire image, including the portion outside of the frame. Notice how much of the image is hidden.

46. With the orange bounding box displayed, use the arrow keys or drag the image with the mouse to move the dolphin to the upper-right corner of the frame. This will expose more of the boat wake in the image.

47. Click outside of the frame to end moving the image viewpoint in the frame.

Captions

Captions are text frames attached to graphic frames to describe or label the images. If the layout changes, the graphic frame can be moved and the caption will follow it.

48. Using the **Selection Tool**, click the graphic frame.

49. Click **Object>Captions>Generate Live Caption** on the **Application** bar. A live caption takes information from the image file and inserts it into a text frame as the caption text. Notice that the text frame is attached below the frame and the caption text is automatically the name of the image file.

50. Applying what you have learned, select the caption text, change the type size to 10 points, change the alignment to center, and apply the Medium Blue color.

51. Edit the caption text to read: Dolphins jump next to the boat.

52. Using the **Selection Tool**, select the graphic frame. Then, resize the frame's height to 12p6. Notice how this has changed not only the size of the graphic frame, but the text frame containing the caption as well, and there is now overset text in the caption frame.

53. Applying what you have learned, resize the caption text frame to 1p6.

Changing an Image Link

A layout project often contains multiple frames. For example, a sales brochure may contain several graphic frames. To speed up the layout process, frames can be quickly and easily copied and pasted. Then, the image in the pasted frame can be updated to a different image.

54. Use the **Selection Tool** to select the graphic frame and caption text frame. To do this, select one of the frames, hold down the [Shift] key, and select the second frame.

55. Applying what you have learned, copy and paste the selected objects. Notice the pasted frames retain the text wrapping of the originals.

56. Drag the pasted frames to the right column vertically aligned with the image in the left column. Use smart guides to help perfectly align the objects.

57. With the new frame selected, click the **Links** panel in the **Panels** bar to expand it. This panel shows all content in the document that is linked to an external file. The image for the currently selected frame is highlighted in the panel.

Go to Link

58. Click the **Go to Link** button at the bottom of the **Links** panel. The view in the document window shifts to the graphic frame in the right column and is centered in the view, and the image is selected with the orange bounding box displayed.

Relink

59. Click the **Relink** button at the bottom of the **Links** panel. A standard open-type dialog box is displayed, which allows you to select a different image file to replace the current image.

60. Navigate to your working folder, and open the Lesson06_Boats01.jpg image file. The dolphin image in the frame is replaced with the new image, as shown in **Figure 6-8.**

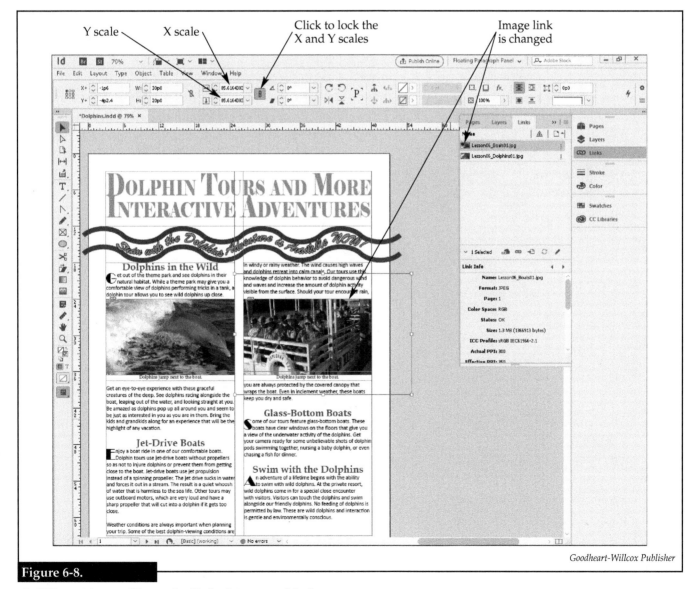

Goodheart-Willcox Publisher

Figure 6-8.

A different image file can be linked to a graphic frame.

**Constrain
Proportional
Scaling**

61. Click the content indicator to display the bounding box for the new image.

62. Click the **Constrain Proportional Scaling** button on the **Control** panel so it is on (depressed or gray). By constraining the proportions, if either the X or the Y value is changed, the other value automatically changes as well to maintain the correct aspect ratio.

63. Click in the **Scale X Percentage:** text box, and enter 63%. Notice the Y value also changes to 63%.

64. Applying what you have learned, position the image so it is centered in the frame.

65. Applying what you have learned, edit the caption to read: Safe and dry boating in all types of weather.

**Wrap around
bounding box**

66. Applying what you have learned, copy and paste the image and caption frames, align the copy to the bottom-right corner of the right column, link the SwimDolphins.jpg image file to the frame, and change the caption to read: Get face-to-face with real dolphins. Proportionally adjust the image to 65 percent, and resize the image and caption frames smaller. Also, change the text wrapping on the graphic frame so the text wraps around the bounding box, as shown in **Figure 6-9.** There should be no overset text in any text frame.

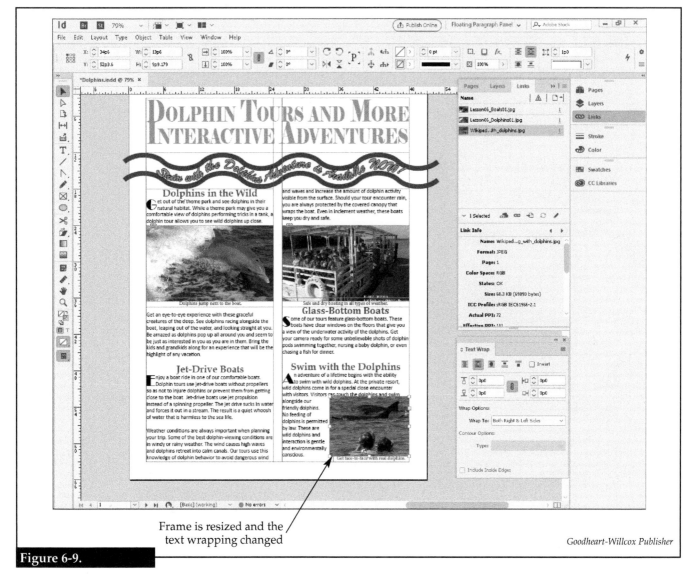

Frame is resized and the
text wrapping changed

Goodheart-Willcox Publisher

Figure 6-9.

One of the options for how text will wrap around a frame is to have the text flow along the side of the frame.

Print PDF Exporting

The document is complete. It is now ready to be sent to a printer or for digital distribution as a PDF. You will create a PDF.

67. Click **File**>**Export...** on the **Application** bar. The **Export** dialog box is displayed, which is a standard save-type dialog box.

68. Navigate to your working folder, change the file name to *LastName*_Print_PDF, change the file type to Adobe PDF (Print), and click the **Save** button. The **Export Adobe PDF** dialog box is displayed, as shown in **Figure 6-10.** This allows you to make adjustments to the output file.

69. Click the **Compatibility:** drop-down arrow, and click **Acrobat 4** in the list. This setting specifies which version of the Acrobat PDF viewer the document is compatible with. It is common to use the lowest possible version number that supports the design of the document to allow for maximum compatibility with PDF readers.

70. Click the **Adobe PDF Preset:** drop-down arrow, and click **Smallest File Size** in the list. Some detail will be lost, but the file will download faster. Notice that the compatibility automatically changed to Acrobat 6 as that is the best match for compatibility.

71. Read the information in the **Description:** text box. This details the best use of this format.

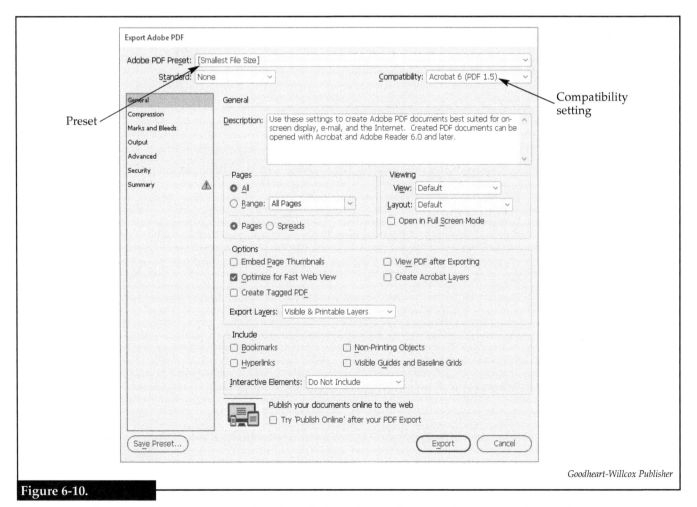

Goodheart-Willcox Publisher

Figure 6-10.

When exporting a PDF, there are several settings that can be made to fine-tune the final file output.

72. Click the **Export** button to finalize the settings and build the PDF.

73. Using your computer's file explorer, navigate to your working folder, and double-click on the *LastName*_Print_PDF file to open it in the default viewer. Depending on your system, this may be Acrobat Reader, Microsoft Edge, or other program.

74. Inspect the PDF to make sure the quality is acceptable. Notice that the images are not quite as clear as the original image files. This is due to the Smallest File Size preset selected when creating the PDF.

75. Inspect the document for proper use of white space. *White space* is any part of the page that does not contain type or a graphic element. It is the "blank" parts of the page. White space is used to add clarity and design balance. A designer should always inspect output to make sure it is readable and to the standard required.

76. Close the PDF, and return to InDesign.

77. Save your work, and close InDesign.

Lesson 6 Review

Vocabulary

In a word processing document or on a sheet of paper, list all of the **key terms** in this lesson. Place each term on a separate line. Then, write a definition for each term using your own words. You will continue to build this terminology dictionary throughout this certification guide.

Review Questions

Answer the following questions. These questions are aligned to questions in the certification exam. Answering these questions will help prepare you to take the exam.

1. What is overset text?

   _____

   _____

2. Briefly describe how to thread text from Text Frame 1 to Text Frame 2.

   _____

   _____

   _____

   _____

3. What type of formatting is a drop cap?

   _____

4. List the three types of frames available in InDesign.

   _____

5. What is text wrapping?

_____

_____

6. What is the purpose of a caption?

_____

_____

7. Why is it important to create a paragraph style instead of manually modifying similar text items in a document?

_____

_____

8. Briefly describe how to change an image link.

_____

_____

_____

_____

9. Which InDesign feature is used to lock the scaling of the X and Y values for an image so the image remains proportional?

_____

10. What is the purpose of the compatibility setting when creating a PDF file?

_____

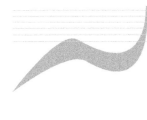

Lesson 7
Digital and Interactive Documents

Objectives

Students will evaluate preflight errors. Students will add links to selected text. Students will explain the process of exporting an interactive PDF.

Reading Material

The Internet and mobile devices have created a huge demand for documents to be created in both print and online formats. Fortunately, InDesign has built-in features that allow a document to be created for online use and to convert a print layout to a digital document. Multimedia features can be added to digital documents, which is not possible with print documents. Some multimedia items include hyperlinks, animations, and page transitions.

A *hyperlink* is a clickable item that takes the user to a location typically outside of the document, but may also be a location within the document. You use hyperlinks all the time when surfing the Internet. Hyperlinks are the foundation of navigating the World Wide Web. Similar to a hyperlink is a bookmark. A *bookmark* navigates to a page within the current document.

Moving items can also be added to the pages in a digital document. An *animation* is a graphic element or object that moves on the page. An animation can be added to provide visual interest or to illustrate something that may be easier to see than read about.

A page transition differs from an animation in that the entire page is involved in the animation. A *page transition* occurs when leaving one page and opening a new page. A page transition may move the entire page, turn the page, or animate a screen pattern to replace one page with another. Page transitions are very similar to slide transitions in PowerPoint.

How to Begin

1. Launch InDesign, and open the *LastName_*Dolphins file. The current print flyer will be converted to an interactive PDF. An *interactive PDF* is a Portable Document Format file that has multimedia elements added.

2. Select the graphic frame containing the image of the boat with the caption.

3. Click **Object>Interactive>Convert to Button** on the **Application** bar. The **Buttons and Forms** panel is displayed, as shown in **Figure 7-1.** A button is an area of the document with which the user can interact. Typically, a button is something that is clicked to activate.

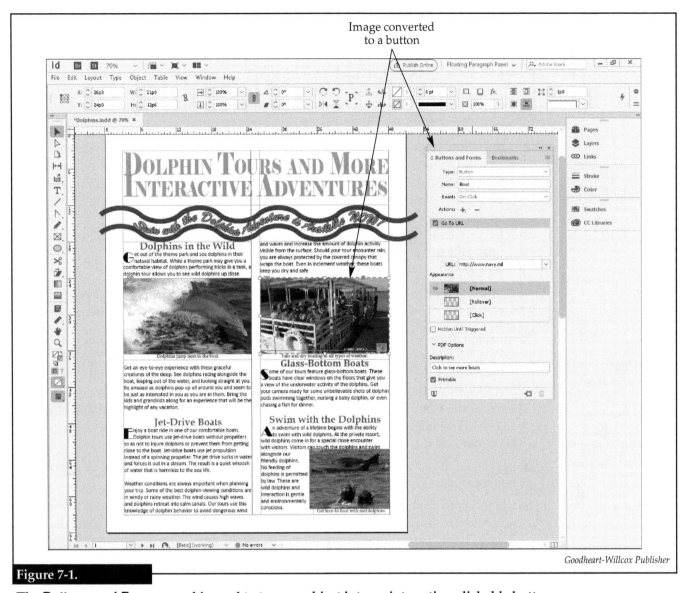

Image converted to a button

Goodheart-Willcox Publisher

Figure 7-1.

The **Buttons and Forms** panel is used to turn an object into an interactive, clickable button.

Option	Meaning
On Release or Tap	When the mouse button is released or the mobile device screen is tapped
On Click	When the cursor is over the button and the mouse button is depressed
On Roll Over	When the cursor moves over the button without the mouse button being pressed
On Roll Off	When the cursor moves from over the button to no longer over it

Goodheart-Willcox Publisher

Figure 7-2.

The options for interaction with a button.

4. Click in the **Name:** text box on the **Button and Forms** panel, and enter Boat.

5. Click the **Event:** drop-down arrow, and click **On Click** in the drop-down list. The event is how the user will activate the button. The options for an event are shown in **Figure 7-2.**

6. Click the plus sign in the **Actions** area to add an action, and click **Go To URL** in the menu that appears. This will allow you to specify a website hyperlink for this button.

7. In the **URL:** text box that appears below the **Actions** area, enter http://www.navy.mil.

8. Click in the **Description:** text box, and enter Click to see more boats. The description provides accessibility to comply with the Americans with Disabilities Act (ADA). To be ADA compliant, alternative text must be provided for each image. This allows screen reader software to read the description to a person with a visual impairment.

9. Dock the **Buttons and Forms** panel at the bottom of the **Panel** bar for easier access later.

10. Applying what you have learned, select the text frame for the main title containing the text *Dolphin Tours and More,* and convert the frame to a button. Name the button Top Text. Program the button to work when clicked by the user and link to the first page of this document. Add a description to be ADA compliant: Click here to return to the start of this document.

Preflight

Preflight is a feature that checks for errors in the InDesign document. The name comes from the checklist that pilots use to make sure everything is in working order before taking off.

TIP

The **Preflight Panel** may not be able to diagnose an error. In this case, the designer must check the preflight errors and make decisions on how to correct them. Not every preflight error is an error that needs to be corrected. Preflight is used to alert the designer to potential errors and allow the designer to make changes at his or her discretion.

11. Applying what you have learned, select the main text frame in the right column, and drag the bottom handle up to make the frame smaller. This will result in overset text.

12. Look at the **Status** bar at the bottom of the InDesign screen. Notice that there is a red dot and the message 1 error, as shown in **Figure 7-3.** This is the live preflight feature, and it detected an error.

13. Click the drop-down arrow to the right of the error message, and click **Preflight Panel** in the menu to open the **Preflight** panel.

14. Click the chevron (>) next to the Text item listed in the **Preflight Panel** to expand that branch. Items in this panel are organized in a tree-like fashion, similar to how a computer's file explorer organizes files. Continue expanding the tree until it is fully expanded. You should see branches for Overset Text and Text Frame.

15. Double-click the Text Frame branch, and InDesign selects the frame with the error.

16. Click the chevron in the **Preflight Panel** to expand the **Info** area of the panel. InDesign tells you how to fix the problem.

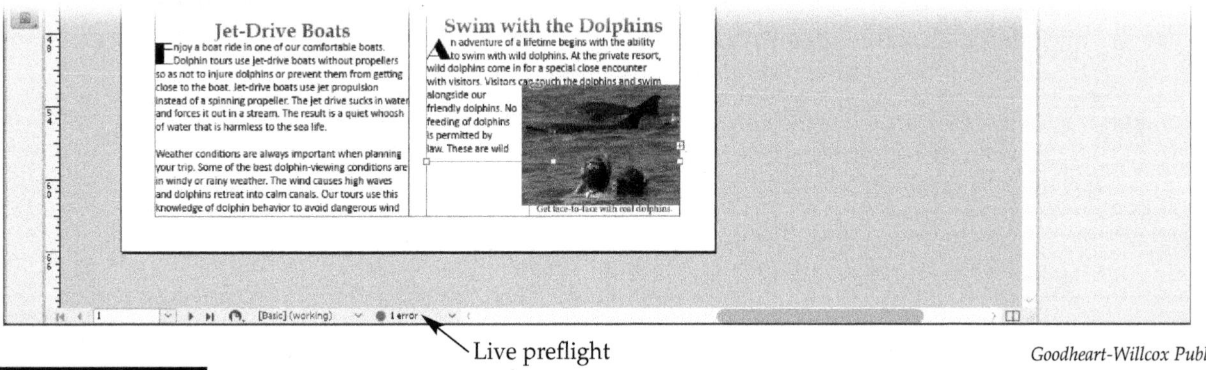

Live preflight

Goodheart-Willcox Publisher

Figure 7-3.

The live preflight is shown in the **Status** bar at the bottom of the InDesign screen.

17. Applying what you have learned, resize the text box in the right column to its original size so there is no longer overset text. Notice the live preflight automatically updates to show the error has been removed. This is reflected in the **Status** bar and in the **Preflight** panel.

18. Close the **Preflight** panel.

Adding Links to Text

19. Applying what you have learned, create a new character style named Hyperlinks. Set the typeface style to italic, and set the color to 100% magenta.

20. Use the **Type Tool** to select the words *weather conditions* at the start of the second paragraph under the Jet Drive Boats heading.

21. Click **Type>Hyperlinks & Cross-References>New Hyperlink...** on the **Application** bar. The **New Hyperlink** dialog box is displayed, as shown in **Figure 7-4.**

22. Click the **Link To:** drop-down arrow. Notice that the hyperlink can link to multiple items as shown in **Figure 7-5.** Click **URL** in the drop-down list. You will assign a web address as the hyperlink.

23. Click in the **URL:** text box in the **Destination** area, and enter http://www.weather.gov.

24. Click **Style:** drop-down arrow in the **Character Style** area, and click **Hyperlinks** in the list. This is the character style you just created.

25. Click the **OK** button to create the hyperlink. Notice the selected text is displayed in the Hyperlinks character style. The hyperlink itself will not be active until the PDF is created.

26. Applying what you have learned, edit the Hyperlinks character style, and change the color to the Medium Blue you created earlier. Notice how all characters in the hyperlink are updated to the new color. This is because the Hyperlinks character style is applied to the entire hyperlink text.

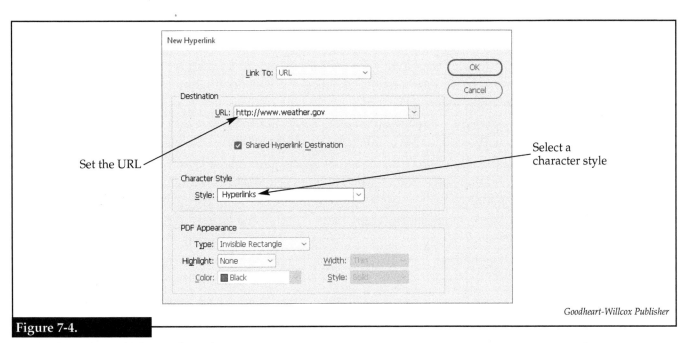

Goodheart-Willcox Publisher

Figure 7-4.

Assigning a hyperlink to selected text.

Option	Meaning
URL	Internet address
File	File located on a server or the local computer
Email	Begins a new e-mail with the address and subject lines filled in
Page	Page within the document
Text Anchor	Specific text anchor or frame within the document
Shared Destination	Link already in the document

Goodheart-Willcox Publisher

Figure 7-5.

A hyperlink can activate one of several types of items.

Exporting as an Interactive PDF

The document is not currently interactive as an InDesign file. To create an interactive document, it must be exported to a PDF file. However, it must be a special type of PDF for the interactive elements to work.

27. Click **File>Export...** on the **Application** bar.

28. In the **Export** dialog box, navigate to your working folder, and change the file name to *LastName*_Dolphin_Interactive_PDF.

29. Click the **Save as Type:** drop-down arrow, and click **Adobe PDF (Interactive)** in the list. Be sure to select the interactive file type.

30. Click the **Save** button.

31. Accept the other default values in the **Export to Interactive PDF** dialog box by clicking the **Export** to create the interactive PDF. If a warning appears indicating there are preflight errors, click the **OK** button to dismiss the warning. When the PDF is built, it will automatically open in the default web browser. Note: Microsoft Edge will *not* allow the hyperlinks to function correctly; use a different browser.

32. With the PDF displayed, hover the cursor over the header text. Notice the cursor changes to a hand to indicate an active hyperlink.

33. Click the boat image button. The browser will navigate to the US Navy website. Use the browser's **Back** button to return to the PDF.

34. Click the hyperlinked text in the Jet Drive Boats section. The browser will navigate to the National Weather Service website.

35. Close all browser windows and the PDF.

36. Using your new skills, export the InDesign document as an InDesign Markup file named *LastName*_Markup saved in your working folder.

37. Using your computer's file explorer, navigate to your working folder, and double-click the *LastName*_Markup file. The document is opened in InDesign as a new tab named Untitled-1.

38. Locate the buttons you created with the header text and the boat image. Notice the ghosted image of a finger pushing a button.

39. Locate the chain icon on top of each image on the document. This indicates the images are linked. Markup shows additional details for the file and is also backward compatible to other InDesign versions going back to InDesign CS4.

40. Close the Untitled-1 document by clicking the **X** on the tab. Do not save if prompted.

41. Save the *LastName*_Dolphins InDesign file, and close InDesign.

Lesson 7 Review

Vocabulary

In a word processing document or on a sheet of paper, list all of the *key terms* in this lesson. Place each term on a separate line. Then, write a definition for each term using your own words. You will continue to build this terminology dictionary throughout this certification guide.

Review Questions

Answer the following questions. These questions are aligned to questions in the certification exam. Answering these questions will help prepare you to take the exam.

1. Compare and contrast hyperlinks and bookmarks.

_____

_____

_____

_____

2. Briefly describe how to convert an object to a button in InDesign.

_____

_____

_____

_____

3. What is the purpose of preflight?

_____

_____

4. What six items can a hyperlink link to?

_____

_____

_____

5. How is an InDesign document saved as an interactive PDF?

_____

_____

_____

_____

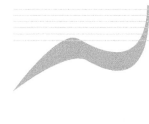

Lesson 8
Digital Document Production

Objectives

Students will rotate objects. Students will describe how to create ruler guides. Students will explain anchor points. Students will compare transparency and opacity. Students will use object styles. Students will construct groups of objects. Students will explain glyphs. Students will convert type to outlines. Students will evaluate an image for public domain usage. Students will animate an image. Students will determine color settings. Students will use the content collector feature. Students will describe document layout options. Students will construct a document package.

Reading Materials

A *copyright* is legal ownership of the work. It protects the creative work by making it illegal for others to copy or use the material without the permission of the owner. As soon as something has been produced in a tangible form, it is automatically copyrighted. This means that if you have an idea for a new character, the idea by itself cannot be copyrighted because an idea is not tangible. You cannot hold, touch, or see an idea. As soon as you draw the character on a sheet of paper, however, that drawing automatically belongs to you and others cannot use it without your permission. The copyright does not need to be registered with the United States Copyright Office, but can be if you choose to do so.

A formal copyright notice consists of the copyright designation, date, and owner. Examples of this include: Copyright 2017 John Smith and ©2017 John Smith. The © symbol means copyright. However, a formal copyright notice or the copyright symbol is not required. Including a notice serves to tell others the work is copyrighted, but if you do not see a notice, you cannot assume the work lacks a copyright. The image or song you find on the Internet most likely is copyrighted. This means you cannot use it unless you get permission from the owner.

According to the *World Intellectual Property Organization (WIPO) Copyright Treaty,* intellectual property, such as music, games, movies, and works of art, is protected worldwide. In the United States, the Digital Millennium Copyright Act (DCMA) enforces the WIPO treaty.

In some limited cases, copyrighted material can be used without the owner's permission under the fair use/fair dealings doctrine. The *fair use/fair dealings doctrine* allows the use of copyrighted material so long as the use is limited to a description or critique of the work. So, a screen capture of a video game used with a description of the game action is not a copyright violation under fair use doctrine. Be aware that the guidelines for claiming usage under fair use/fair dealings doctrine are very strict.

When a creative work has been around for a long time, it is placed in the public domain. *Public domain* applies to any work for which the copyright term has expired. It means any and all copyrights on the work have been removed. There is no more legal protection preventing duplication, and the work is free to use. The time period after which a creative work falls into the public domain varies. For example, in the United States, any work published after 1978 passes into the public domain 70 years after the creator has died.

As a digital artist, it is a best practice to research any image you intend to use to understand what rights are assigned to the image. It is your responsibility to contact the owner and get permission to use any creative work that is not specifically marked as "free use" or "public domain." Be sure to record and save any documentation granting you permission to use the image. Using an image or other copyrighted work beyond the scope of the license or granted permission is *copyright infringement.* Copyright infringement can carry both criminal and civil penalties, including fines and incarceration.

A *trademark* is similar to a copyright, but it is legal ownership of a word, phrase, symbol, or design that identifies the unique source of a product. Designating the logo as trademarked provides legal protection to the design. The ™ symbol indicates that the trademark has not been registered with the United States Patent and Trademark Office. The ® symbol indicates the trademark has been registered.

How to Begin

1. Launch Adobe InDesign Creative Cloud.
2. Applying what you have learned, create a new document using the web intent. Accept all default settings.
3. Applying what you have learned, save the document as *LastName*_Digital in your working folder.

Object Rotation

Rectangle

4. Applying what you have learned, draw a rectangle on the page. Set the reference point to the center, and change the size of the rectangle to two inches wide and high. What are the dimensions in pixels (px)?

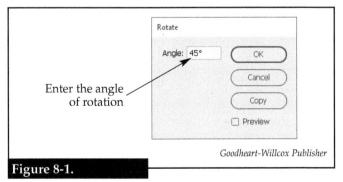

Enter the angle of rotation

Goodheart-Willcox Publisher

Figure 8-1.

Rotating an object. Angles are measured counterclockwise in InDesign.

5. Drag the rectangle to the center of the document. Use smart guides to help center the rectangle.
6. Click **Object>Transform>Rotate…** on the **Application** bar. The **Rotate** dialog box is displayed, as shown in **Figure 8-1.**
7. Click in the **Angle:** text box, enter 45, and click the **OK** button. Angles are measured counterclockwise in InDesign.

Ruler Guide Placement

Ruler guides, or guidelines, are helper objects. They are straight lines that extend across the page, either vertically or horizontally.

8. Click on the top ruler, and drag downward to pull out a ruler guide. Continue dragging downward until the value in the **Y:** text box on the **Control** panel is about 200 px. When you release the mouse button, a horizontal ruler guide is created.

9. Using the **Selection Tool**, click the guide to select it. An unselected guide is cyan. A selected guide is blue.

10. Change the value in the **Y:** text box on the **Control** panel to 250 px.

11. Click any blank area of the document to deselect the guide.

12. Applying what you have learned, create another horizontal ruler guide at Y = 150.

13. Click the left-hand ruler, and drag to the right until the value in the **X:** text box on the **Control** panel is 250 px. When you release the mouse button, a vertical ruler guide is created.

14. Applying what you have learned, create another vertical ruler guide at X = 550.

Anchor Points

Anchor points are nodes on a path. When you created the rectangle, it included four anchor points, one at each corner. Anchor points can be added and removed from a path.

15. Applying what you have learned, change the zoom level to about 250 percent and center the top corner of the rectangle in the view.

16. Click the **Add Anchor Point Tool** button in the **Tools** panel.

Add Anchor Point Tool

17. Single-click where the edge of the square and the horizontal guide at Y = 250 intersect. Do this at both intersections. An anchor point is added to the path (square) in two locations.

18. Click the **Direct Selection Tool** button in the **Tools** panel.

Direct Selection Tool

19. Click the new anchor point on the right side of the rectangle, and drag it to the intersection of the guides at X = 550, Y = 150, as shown in **Figure 8-2.**

20. Move the new anchor point on the left side of the rectangle to the intersection of the guides at X = 250, Y = 150.

21. Applying what you have learned, create four new ruler guides at the following locations.

Vertical	Horizontal
X = 480	Y = 100
X = 180	Y = 200

22. Click the **Convert Direction Point Tool** button in the **Tools** panel. This tool changes anchor points from corners to curves and vice versa.

Convert Direction Point Tool

23. Click the right-hand anchor point, and drag upward to the intersection of the guides at X = 480, Y = 100. The anchor point is converted to a curve, and as you drag a handle is pulled out from the point. A Bézier curve will extend and the point will round out.

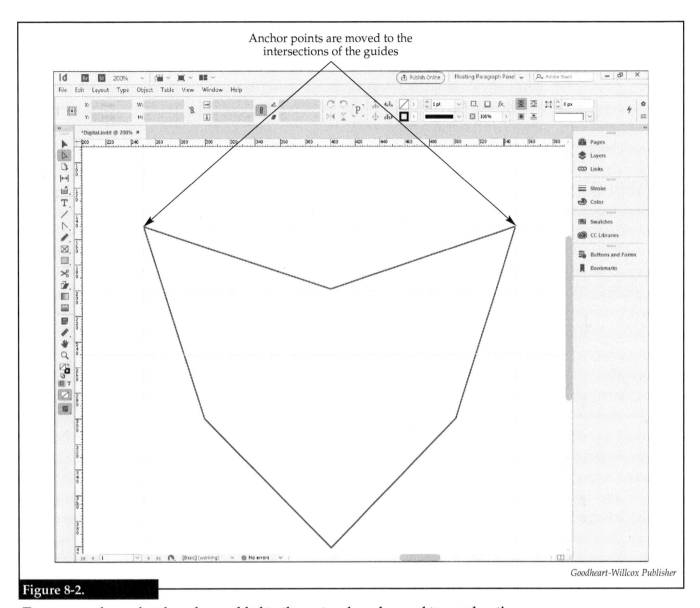

Figure 8-2.

Two new anchor points have been added to the rectangle and moved to new locations.

24. Applying what you have learned, convert the left-hand anchor point to a curve and drag the handle to the intersection of the guides at X = 180, Y = 200. This should create a heart shape.

25. Click **View>Grids & Guides>Delete All Guides on Spread** on the **Application** bar. All of the ruler guides you added are deleted.

26. Applying what you have learned, change the zoom level to fit the page in the window.

27. Select the heart shape, and click **Object>Transform>Scale...** on the **Application** bar. The **Scale** dialog box is displayed.

28. Click the **Constrain proportions for scaling** button (chain icon), enter 50 in either text box, and click the **OK** button. By clicking the **Constrain proportions for scaling** button, changing either the X or the Y scaling factor automatically changes the other one to match.

Transparency and Opacity

Transparency is a measure of how see-through an object is. The opposite of transparency is opacity. An object that is fully opaque has no transparency, while an object that is fully transparent has no opacity.

TIP
The colors in the document are based on RGB because the default settings for the web intent result in a document based on RGB color.

29. Select the heart shape.

30. Applying what you have learned, fill the shape with the RGB Red color.

31. Applying what you have learned, change the stroke color to None.

32. Click **Object>Effects>Transparency...** on the **Application** bar. The **Effects** dialog box is displayed, as shown in **Figure 8-3.**

33. Click in the **Opacity:** text box, enter 50, and click the **OK** button. The object is made semitransparent. In this case, since there are no objects behind the heart to show through, the effect appears as if the red has been changed to pink, but what you are seeing is the white page showing through the heart.

34. Applying what you have learned, draw a diagonal line starting at coordinates (500, 150) and extending to coordinates (320, 300). Use the settings in the **Control** panel to help properly position the line.

35. Applying what you have learned, use the **Stroke** panel to change the weight to 4 points, the start to a barbed arrow point, and the end to a bar.

36. With the line selected, click **Object>Arrange>Send to Back** on the **Application** bar. The arrow should be visible through the heart.

Line Tool

Object Style

An object style is much like a paragraph or character style. Styles are collections of settings that can be easily applied again later. An object style ensures all objects that should look the same indeed have identical settings.

37. Select the heart.

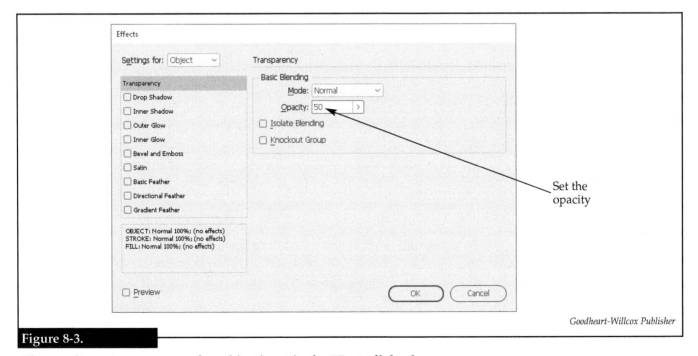

Goodheart-Willcox Publisher

Figure 8-3.

The opacity or transparency of an object is set in the **Effects** dialog box.

Create new style

38. Click **Window>Styles>Object Styles** in the **Application** bar to open the **Object Styles** panel.
39. Click the **Create new style** button at the bottom of the **Object Styles** panel.
40. Applying what you have learned, name the new style Red, See-Through, and then apply the style to the heart.

Grouping

Grouping allows individual objects to be combined to act as a single object. However, the objects are not permanently combined. They can be separated into the individual objects if needed.

TIP
You can drag a selection box around objects to select multiple items.

41. Activate the **Selection Tool**, hold down the [Shift] key, and click the arrow. Both the heart and the arrow should be selected. The [Shift] allows you to select multiple objects at the same time.
42. Click **Object>Group** on the **Application** bar. The two objects are combined into a single object. If you try to move one object, both move in unison.
43. Click **Object>Ungroup** on the **Application** bar. Now the objects can be moved individually.
44. Applying what you have learned, undo any movements you made, and then group the heart and arrow.

Glyphs

Glyphs are text symbols, such as the © and ® symbols. These are not part of the normal keyboard characters. Glyphs are inserted using the **Glyphs** panel.

45. Applying what you have learned, draw a rectangle that is 728 pixels wide and 80 pixels in height. Align the rectangle to the top margin of the page centered left-to-right. Apply the Red, See-Through object style so it matches the heart.
46. Applying what you have learned, draw a text frame that is the same size as the rectangle at the top of the page. Add the text Valentine's Day to the frame. Change the typeface to Arial, the style to bold, the size to 72 points, and center align the text.
47. Place the text insertion point after the Y in *Day*.
48. Click **Type>Glyphs** on the **Application** bar. The **Glyphs** panel is displayed, as shown in **Figure 8-4.** Notice that the typeface and style listed at the bottom of the panel match the *Valentine's Day* text (Arial, bold).
49. Click the **Show:** drop-down arrow, which is currently set to **Entire Font**, and click **Symbols** in the drop-down list. This part of the typeface collection is where you will find glyphs such as the © and ® symbols.
50. Using the drop-down list at the bottom of the panel, change the typeface to Webdings.
51. Click the **Show:** drop-down arrow, and click **Entire Font** in the list so all characters in the typeface will be displayed.
52. Locate the heart glyph, and double-click it. The glyph is added to the text box where the insertion point is located.
53. Select the heart glyph in the text box.

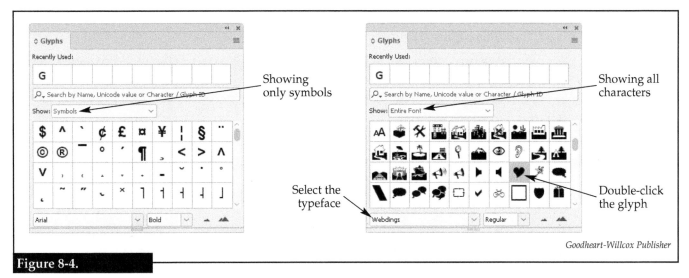

Showing only symbols

Showing all characters

Select the typeface

Double-click the glyph

Goodheart-Willcox Publisher

Figure 8-4.

Symbols are called glyphs in InDesign and are inserted using the **Glyphs** panel.

Superscript

TIP
When the V is converted to outlines, notice the last part of the word *Valentine's* is underlined in red to indicate a misspelled word. The V is no longer type, thus InDesign only sees *alentine's* as the word.

Direct Selection Tool

Delete Anchor Point Tool

54. Click the **Superscript** button in the character formatting options on the **Control** panel. The heart becomes smaller and is shifted up from the baseline.

55. Applying what you have learned, cut and paste the superscript heart to replace the apostrophe (') in the word *Valentine's.*

56. Drag the text frame down until the text is visually centered top-to-bottom in the rectangle.

Outline Text

Type can be converted into vector objects. This process is called creating outlines. Once converted to outlines, the vector objects can be manipulated by dragging the path handles. However, the objects are no longer type, they are images.

57. Select the V in *Valentine's,* and click **Type>Create Outlines** on the **Application** bar. The V is converted into a vector object.

58. Deselect the text frame.

59. Change the zoom level to 600 percent, and center the V in view.

60. Click the **Direct Selection Tool** button in the **Tools** panel, move the cursor over the V, and click to show the handles for each node in the outline of the character.

61. Click the **Delete Anchor Point Tool** button in the **Tools** panel.

62. Click each of the two anchor points on the inside top of the V to delete them. This will create a sharp-pointed V, as shown in **Figure 8-5.**

63. Applying what you have learned, convert the remaining two top anchor points of the V to curves, and modify the handles to create a heart shape.

64. Applying what you have learned, refine the shape to finalize the heart shape.

65. Applying what you have learned, set the fill color to white and the stroke color to RGB Red.

66. Change the zoom level so the page fits in the window.

67. Draw a text frame to fill the space between the red rectangle and the remainder of the page within the margins.

68. Applying what you have learned, fill the text frame with placeholder text.

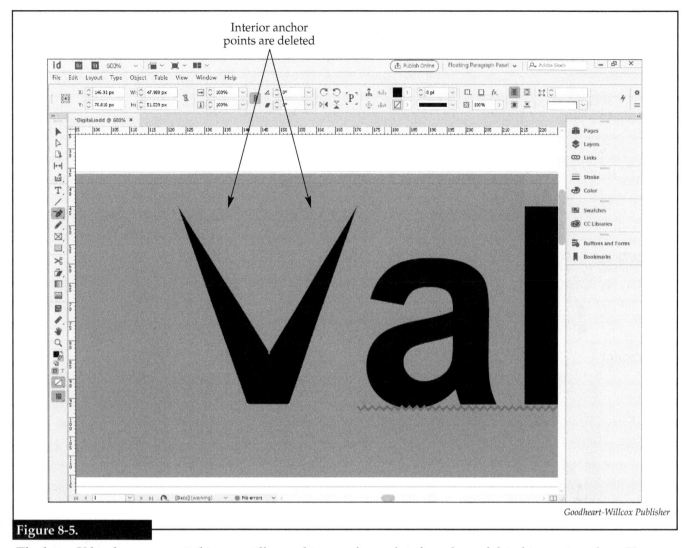

Interior anchor
points are deleted

Goodheart-Willcox Publisher

Figure 8-5.

The letter V has been converted to an outline and two anchor points have been deleted to create a sharp V.

69. Activate the **Selection Tool**, click outside the page, and drag a box that touches the heart and arrow. The heart, arrow, and large text frame will be selected.

70. Applying what you have learned, set the text wrapping to wrap around the object shape. The text in the large text frame should follow the edges of the heart and the arrow.

TIP
Always keep a record of where images came from and document the usage permissions. One way to do this is to create a screen capture of the page where the image was and include the part indicating the license.

Public Domain Image

71. Launch a web browser, and conduct an image search for an illustration of a broken heart. Modify the image search results to display only public domain images. The method for doing this will depend on which search engine you use. For a Google image search, click **Tools**, then **Usage Rights**, and select **Labeled for reuse**, as shown in **Figure 8-6.** In Bing, click **Filter**, then **License**, and select **Public domain**.

72. Find a broken heart image and select it to preview it. The image should have a faint checkerboard visible in the white area to indicate that it is transparent outside of the heart. Right-click on the image, and save it to your working folder as Broken Heart.

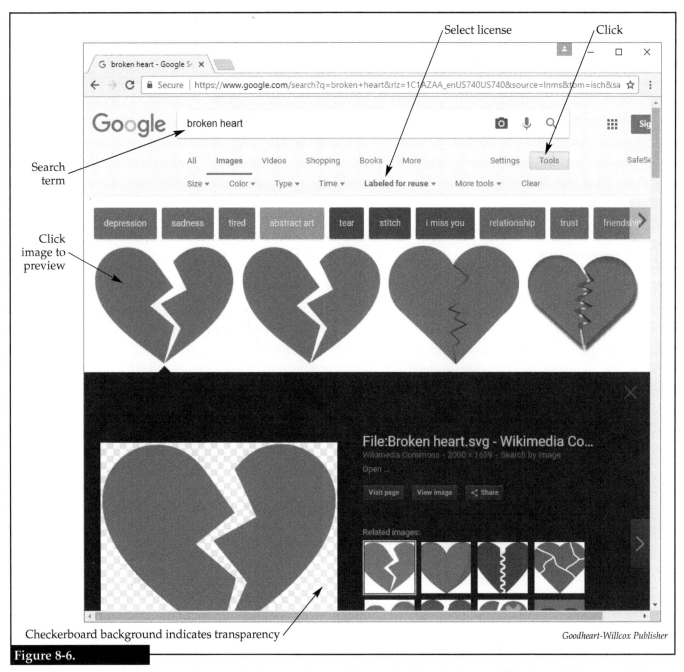

Goodheart-Willcox Publisher

Figure 8-6.

Searching for a public domain image of a heart. The specific method for finding public domain images will vary based on which search engine is being used.

73. Applying what you have learned, place the Broken Heart image file anywhere on the page in InDesign.

74. Applying what you have learned, proportionally scale the image as needed so it is about one-quarter of the page.

75. Position the Broken Heart image at the bottom-left corner of the page.

76. With the Broken Heart image selected, click **Object>Clipping Path>Options...** on the **Application** bar. The **Clipping Path** dialog box is displayed.

77. In the **Clipping Path** dialog box, click the **Type:** drop-down arrow, click **Detect Edges**, in the list, and then click the **OK** button to apply the clipping path with the default settings. A *clipping path* is a line surrounding an area of an image or object outside of which the image or object is hidden.

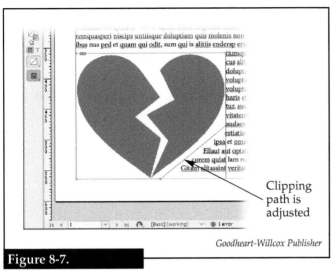

Clipping path is adjusted

Goodheart-Willcox Publisher

Figure 8-7.

The clipping path has been modified to create an angled cut in the text.

78. Applying what you have learned, add text wrapping around the object shape.

79. Using the **Direct Selection Tool**, move the anchor points of the frame to adjust the shape of the text wrap to an angle at the bottom of the broken heart, as shown in **Figure 8-7**. Add anchor points as needed to achieve the desired effect.

Animated Images

Web-based and digital documents can include animations. Animated images are those images that have movement or visual changes. In InDesign, the controls for animations are contained in the **Animation** panel.

80. Click **Window>Interactive>Animation** on the **Application** bar. The **Animation** panel is displayed.

81. Dock the **Animation** panel at the bottom of the **Panel** bar, and leave it expanded.

82. Select the Broken Heart image. The name appears in the **Name:** section of the **Animation** panel.

83. Click the **Preset:** drop-down arrow in the **Animation** panel, and click **Rotate>Rotate 90° CCW** in the drop-down menu. A preview plays at the top of the **Animation** panel to show what the effect will look like.

84. Click the **Event(s):** drop-down arrow, and click **On Click (Self)** in the drop-down menu. By default, the animation will start when the page loads. The setting you just applied will have it start when the image is clicked.

85. Look at the **Event(s):** section. Are two events listed? If so, click the **Event(s):** drop-down arrow, and uncheck the **On Page Load** option, as shown in **Figure 8-8**.

86. Click **Window>Interactive>SWF Preview** on the **Application** bar. The **SWF Preview** panel is displayed. This panel provides a preview of any animation in the document as it should appear in the interactive document output.

87. Click the Broken Heart image in the **SWF Preview** panel to see it rotate in the preview.

88. Close the **SWF Preview** panel.

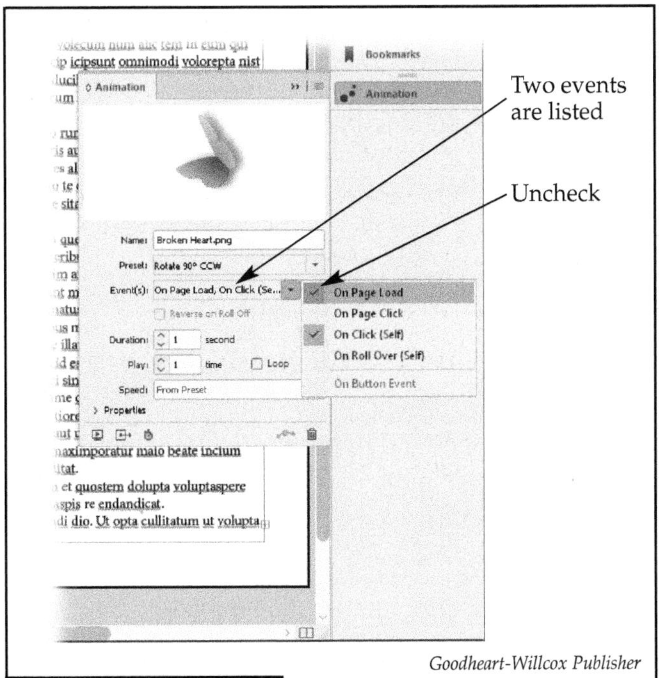

Two events are listed

Uncheck

Goodheart-Willcox Publisher

Figure 8-8.

If the On Page Load event is listed, uncheck it in the drop-down menu.

Color Settings

Color settings can be modified in InDesign. This is usually done to better represent the intended output. In this case, the document is an interactive web-based document, so the colors should reflect the intended output.

89. Click **Edit>Color Settings...** on the **Application** bar. The **Color Settings** dialog box is displayed.

90. Click the **Settings:** drop-down arrow, and click **North America Web/Internet** in the list. The other settings in the dialog box are changed to correlate to this preset setting.

91. Click the **OK** button to update the color settings.

Content Collector

Content Collector Tool

The **Content Collector Tool** allows the designer to collect copies of objects in a collection tray and later use the **Content Placer Tool** to paste them in other areas of the document.

92. Click the **Content Collector Tool** button in the **Tools** panel. The **Collector Conveyor** panel is displayed, as shown in **Figure 8-9.** Currently, a message is displayed indicating there is no content collected.

93. With the **Content Collector Tool** active, click the Broken Heart image. The image is added to the **Collector Conveyor** panel.

Content Placer Tool

94. Click the **Content Placer Tool** button at the bottom of the **Content Conveyor** panel. This tool is used to place the content that is currently selected in the **Content Conveyor** panel into the document. Notice that the Broken Heart image has a blue border, which indicates it is selected.

TIP

The **Content Placer Tool** button is also located in the **Tools** panel.

95. Click in the bottom-right corner of the document to place the copy of the Broken Heart image there. Notice how the **Content Conveyor** panel is now empty. The copy has been moved from the panel into the document.

96. Close the **Collector Conveyor** panel by clicking the close button (**X**).

97. With the second Broken Heart image selected, click **Object>Transform>Flip Horizontal** on the **Application** bar. The image is mirrored.

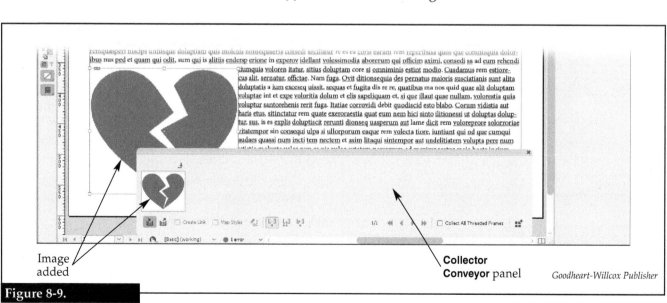

Image added

Collector Conveyor panel

Goodheart-Willcox Publisher

Figure 8-9.

The **Collector Conveyor** panel is a container for holding content to be used later.

Document Layout Options

Layout options apply settings to the entire page or selected pages. If you are creating a report or a book, setting up guides can also help create a table of contents page by providing a grid to which text frames can be aligned.

98. Applying what you have learned, add a second page to the document.

99. Click **File>Document Setup…** on the **Application** bar. In the **Document Setup** dialog box, add a 0p6 bleed to all sides of the document.

100. Click **Layout>Create Guides…** on the **Application** bar. The **Create Guides** dialog box is displayed, as shown in **Figure 8-10.**

101. Modify the settings to have three rows and four columns of guides that are all 15 pixels apart from each other. Apply the guides to fit between the margins. Click the **OK** button to create the guides.

102. Applying what you have learned, use the Internet to find four public domain images of hearts, and place them in the top row of the grid pattern.

103. Use the **Content Collector Tool** to copy all four images to the **Content Conveyor** panel.

104. Use the **Content Placer Tool** to paste the images in a different order on the bottom row of the page.

105. Applying what you have learned, draw a text frame to cover the entire middle row, and add placeholder text to it.

106. Applying what you have learned, delete all guides from the spread.

Package the Document

Packaging a document saves all of the fonts and linked images to ensure they are included in the document before it is sent to a printer or other partner. This ensures the document can be opened by someone else without missing items that are not installed on the other person's computer. A report is also created with the package showing what is included.

107. Click **File>Package…** on the **Application** bar. The **Package** dialog box is displayed, as shown in **Figure 8-11.** It may take a few seconds for the dialog box to open as InDesign gathers information.

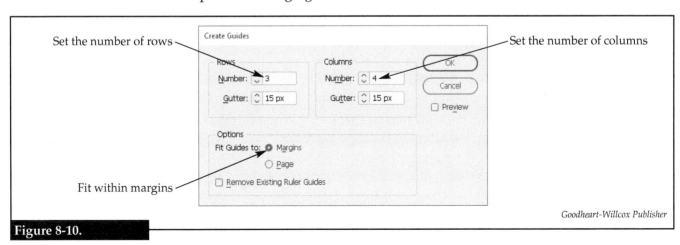

Set the number of rows

Set the number of columns

Fit within margins

Goodheart-Willcox Publisher

Figure 8-10.

Creating a layout of guides of three rows and four columns.

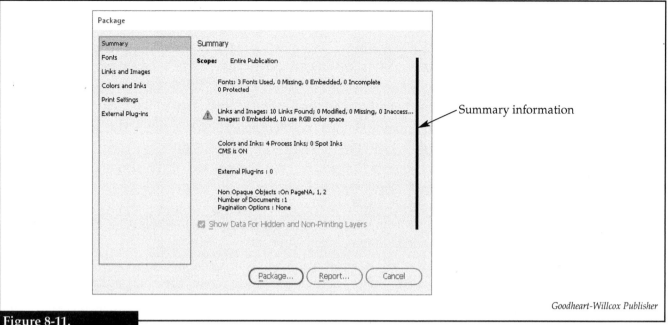

Summary information

Goodheart-Willcox Publisher

Figure 8-11.

The summary displayed when creating a package of the document.

108. Click **Summary** on the left side of the dialog box, and examine the summary on the right. Notice it lists three typefaces used.

109. Click **Fonts** on the left side. All typefaces used in the document that will be included in the package are displayed on the right. If the printer does not have the Webdings typeface installed, the package includes the correct typeface so the document will appear correct.

110. Click **Colors and Inks** on the left. All inks needed, including any spot colors or custom inks, to correctly print the document are listed on the right.

111. Click the **Package...** button at the bottom of the dialog box. If a message appears asking you to save the document, click the **Save** button. Then, the **Printing Instructions** dialog box is displayed, as shown in **Figure 8-12.**

112. Click in the **Filename:** text box, and enter Valentine.txt.

113. Click in the **Contact:** text box, and enter your name.

114. Click in the **Instructions:** text box, and enter Call me if you have any questions.

115. Click the **Continue** button. A save-type dialog box is displayed with options for the package.

116. Navigate to your working folder.

117. Click in the **Folder Name** text box, and enter Valentines Project. The package will be saved in this subfolder within your working folder.

118. Check the **View Report** check box. When this is checked, the report will be displayed after the package is created.

119. Click the **Package** button. A warning is displayed regarding the copyright of typefaces (fonts). Read the statement, and the click the **OK** button. You may receive another warning regarding overset text. If so, click the **OK** button to ignore the error. The package is created, which may take a few seconds, and the report text file is displayed.

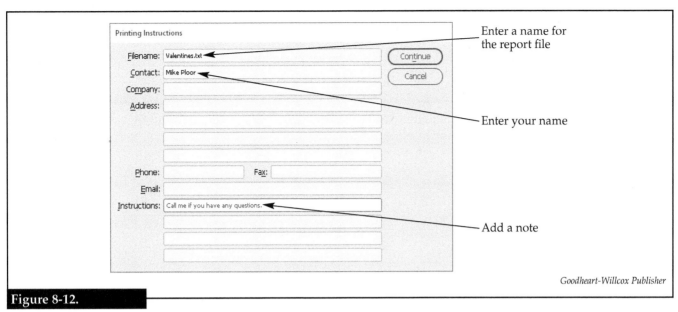

Figure 8-12.

The **Printing Instructions** dialog box is used to provide information about the package that will be included in the report.

120. Inspect the report to see that the typefaces are listed and only the four process colors are used. Then, close the report.

121. Save the InDesign document, and close InDesign.

Lesson 8 Review

Vocabulary

In a word processing document or on a sheet of paper, list all of the *key terms* in this lesson. Place each term on a separate line. Then, write a definition for each term using your own words. You will continue to build this terminology dictionary throughout this certification guide.

Review Questions

Answer the following questions. These questions are aligned to questions in the certification exam. Answering these questions will help prepare you to take the exam.

1. In which direction are angles measured in InDesign?

_____

2. Which tool is used to change an anchor point from a corner to a curve?

_____

3. Briefly describe how to set the opacity of an image.

_____

_____

_____

_____

4. How are the ends of a line changed to an arrow or bar?

_____

_____

_____

5. Which panel is used to save the formatting settings for an object so the settings can be reused on other objects?

_____

6. What are symbols such as copyright and trademark called in InDesign?

_____

7. Briefly explain how to convert type to outlines.

_____

_____

_____

8. Which type of images have no copyright and do not require permission to use?

_____

9. What is committed if you use an image beyond what is permitted by the image license?

_____

10. How can a clipping path be configured to detect the edges of an image?

_____

_____

_____

11. What is the difference between the **On Click (Self)** and **On Page Load** animation options?

_____

_____

12. Which panel is used to animate an object rotating 90 degrees clockwise?

_____

13. Which tool is used to copy an image into the **Content Conveyor** panel?

_____

14. Briefly describe how to place guides in a pattern for the entire page.

_____

_____

_____

15. How can a grid of guides help lay out a table of contents page for a book?

_____

_____

Answers

Lesson 1

Review Questions

1. layout
2. foundry type
3. kerning
4. tracking
5. leading
6. A typeface is a collection of letters, numbers, and symbols all of the same design, while a font is a set of characters within a typeface of one specific style and size.
7. sans serif
8. sans serif
9. The typeface will be displayed in a substituted font.
10. 72
11. An invisible line on which type is placed.
12. plain text (TXT)
13. Rich Text Format (RTF)
14. How easy or hard it is for a person to read the text.
15. Use of two or more typefaces in the same document that are too similar to each other.

Lesson 2

Figure 2-7

1. **Selection Tool**
2. **Direct Selection Tool**
3. **Page Tool**
4. **Gap Tool**
5. **Content Collector Tool**
6. **Content Placer Tool**
7. **Type Tool**
8. **Type on a Path Tool**
9. **Line Tool**
10. **Pen Tool**
11. **Add Anchor Point Tool**
12. **Delete Anchor Point Tool**
13. **Convert Direction Point Tool**
14. **Pencil Tool**
15. **Smooth Tool**
16. **Erase Tool**
17. **Rectangle Frame Tool**
18. **Ellipse Frame Tool**
19. **Polygon Frame Tool**
20. **Rectangle Tool**
21. **Ellipse Tool**
22. **Polygon Tool**
23. **Scissors Tool**
24. **Free Transform Tool**
25. **Rotate Tool**
26. **Scale Tool**
27. **Shear Tool**
28. **Gradient Swatch Tool**
29. **Gradient Feather Tool**
30. **Note Tool**
31. **Color Theme Tool**
32. **Eyedropper Tool**
33. **Measure Tool**
34. **Hand Tool**
35. **Zoom Tool**

Figure 2-8

1. **Pages**
2. **Layers**
3. **Links**
4. **Stroke**
5. **Color**
6. **Swatches**
7. **CC Libraries**

Review Questions

1. Objects, images, templates, and snippets.

2. **Facing Pages**

3. The trim is where the edge of the paper will be when it is cut to size after printing. It is shown in InDesign as a black rectangle.

4. Select the text frame, and then click **Type>Fill with Placeholder Text** on the **Application** bar.

5. Click and hold the flyout button to display the flyout, and then click the tool to use in the flyout.

6. Layers are like invisible sheets of paper stacked on top of each other. Shapes placed on the top layers will appear in front of shapes on the bottom layers.

7. The **Toggles visibility** button (eye).

8. It locks the layer and prevents changes from being made to it.

9. Double-click on the layer name in the **Layers** panel to open the **Layer Options** dialog box and enter the new name there, or single-click twice on the layer name in the **Layers** panel and rename the layer.

10. Edit the master page, add a text box and select it, and click **Type>Insert Special Character>Markers>Current Page Number** on the **Application** bar.

11. Select the page in the panel, click the **Edit Page Size** button at the bottom of the panel, and select the new size in the drop-down menu or click **Custom...** in the menu to change the page size in the **Custom Page Size** dialog box.

12. Drag and drop the page thumbnail into the desired spread.

13. Click and hold the top bar of the panel, drag the panel to the **Panels** bar, and drop it in the location.

14. Drag the panel away from the **Panels** bar, and then click the close button on the panel.

15. Along the top and left side of the document window.

Lesson 3

Review Questions

1. process

2. CMYK

3. vector

4. Raster images are composed of colored dots at specified locations, while vector images are composed of elements recorded by their mathematical definitions.

5. The alpha channel allows for a masking color, which is a single shade of a color that determines areas of transparency in the image.

6. The process of converting a vector image into a raster image.

7. Applying the most appropriate resolution and file compression, which is a process known as optimizing.

8. PNG-24

9. The image is dithered, and the software creates a color through interpolation.

10. SVG

11. EPS

12. JPEG

13. TIFF

14. 576

15. Bicubic for enlargement.

Lesson 4

8. 1/2 inch from the top and left edges

9. 7 1/2 inches wide by 1 1/2 inches high

66. 1p6

Review Questions

1. Use the **Type Tool** and click the rectangular frame.
2. **Character Formatting Controls** and **Paragraph Formatting Controls**
3. Uppercase characters that are smaller than the normal uppercase characters.
4. **Horizontal Scale**
5. By changing the **Vertical Scale** property on the **Control** panel.
6. **Baseline Shift**
7. When type is selected, in the **Character Formatting Controls** in the **Control** panel.
8. **Stroke** panel
9. smart guides
10. **Pencil Tool**
11. Draw a path, then using the **Type on a Path Tool**, click the path and add the text.
12. Click the **Create New Style** button at the bottom of the **Paragraph Styles** panel.
13. The properties of the text are automatically applied to the new style.
14. Click the style name in the **Paragraph Styles** panel.
15. Click **Layout>Margins and Columns...** on the **Application** bar, and then set the number of columns in the **Margins and Columns** dialog box.

Lesson 5

Review Questions

1. Client-centric design principles; client, target audience, and industry standards.
2. Preproduction, production, testing, and publication.
3. Selecting the best team members for the job, identifying the tasks, and determining deadlines for that project.
4. Client goals and target market.
5. Using little or no text, including fantasy characters, and applying bright colors.
6. Interviews and surveys.
7. Demographics help segment the population into smaller groups that have similarities, which allows the designer to create items to appeal to the target market.
8. deadline
9. scope creep
10. A drive-through restaurant will likely have a medium to low formality; examples will vary.
11. 1) During preproduction, use sketches and mockups to help the client visualize the designs you are planning to create. 2) Make notes on the sketches to track the changes and approval of the client. 3) Update the client on the overall progress and get approval on any completed artwork.
12. Raster images, because each point of color is recorded.
13. **Proof Colors**, or soft-proof mode
14. Adobe Creative Cloud and Adobe Bridge.
15. A linked image maintains a connection to the original image file, whereas an embedded image is a copy of the image with no link to the original file.

Lesson 6

38. 21p9 wide by 12p0 high

Review Questions

1. The overflow text that will not fit within the text frame.
2. Click the outport on Text Frame 1, and then click Text Frame 2.
3. Paragraph
4. Text, graphic, and unassigned.
5. How the text flows around a frame.
6. To label an image.

7. Use of styles ensures similar items in the document will all have the same treatment.

8. Select the graphic frame, click the **Relink** button at the bottom of the **Links** panel, and select the new image file.

9. The **Constrain Proportional Scaling** button on the **Control** panel.

10. To determine which PDF readers are able to read the file.

Lesson 7

Review Questions

1. Both hyperlinks and bookmarks are navigational tools. A hyperlink takes the user to a location outside or within the document, while a bookmark takes a user to a page within the same document.

2. Select the object, and click **Object>Interactive>Convert to Button** on the **Application** bar. Then, in the **Buttons and Forms** panel, specify what the button will do.

3. It is a feature that checks for errors in the InDesign document.

4. URL, file, e-mail, page, text anchor, and shared destination (link already in document).

5. Click **File>Export…** on the **Application** bar, and in the **Export** dialog box, select **Adobe PDF (Interactive)** in the **Save as Type:** drop-down list.

Lesson 8

4. 144 by 144

Review Questions

1. counterclockwise

2. **Convert Direction Point Tool**

3. Click **Object>Effects>Transparency…** on the **Application** bar, and then set the opacity in the **Effects** dialog box.

4. Use the **Stroke** panel to change the start and end settings.

5. The **Object Styles** panel.

6. glyphs

7. Select the text, and then click **Type>Create Outlines** on the **Application** bar.

8. public domain

9. copyright infringement

10. Select the image, click **Object>Clipping Path>Options…** on the **Application** bar, and set the **Type:** drop-down list in the **Clipping Path** dialog box to **Detect Edges**.

11. With the **On Click (Self)** option, the animation will begin only when the object is clicked. With the **On Page Load** option, the animation will begin as soon as the page is loaded.

12. The **Animation** panel.

13. **Content Collector Tool**

14. Click **Layout>Create Guides…** on the **Application** bar, and then make the settings in the **Create Guides** dialog box.

15. By providing a grid to which text frames can be aligned.